LINK TUIT

A System to Organize Your Life

Using MS Word
and hyperlinks –
organize your
professional and
personal life.

THOMAS M.
MALAFARINA

Printed in the United States of America

FIRST EDITION

ISBN: 978-1-952352-02-7
eBook: 978-1-952352-03-4

Published by:

Crave Press

www.cravepress.com

Table Of Contents

Introduction

Link-Tuit — a catchy name, a fancy logo you might say. And a slogan that seems to promise things you might not believe it can deliver: "A System to Organize Your Life." Seriously? That's a rather bold claim. So, you might ask, what is Link-Tuit and how exactly is it going to help organize my life?

Before we get into that, let me introduce myself. My name is Thomas M. Malafarina. (Tom to my friends, and if you're reading this, you qualify.) I have earned my living for the past forty plus years in the world of CNC (computer numerical control) and CAD/CAM (computer aided design/computer aided manufacturing) programming. My profession requires me to have access to tons of pertinent technical data at a moment's notice. I also am an author of more than fifteen publish books of horror fiction and well over 150 published short stories. I am a musician, playing in two different local blues bands. In addition, I do artwork and cartooning. As if that is not enough, I am also a husband, a father, a grandfather, and I enjoy vacationing as well as many home improvement projects.

The reason I mention this is that I am often asked by friends how in the world I manage to juggle all these different pastimes at once. My answer is generally "time management," but there is more to it than that. I must be organized in both my professional and personal life, and I have to be able to find what I need to find immediately. When I was in my twenties and thirties, I could rely heavily on my memory to get by. But by the time I was thirty-five or so, the amount of information I was required to juggle began to grow exponentially.

I had tons of technical manuals and documentation as well as mountains of personal notes, some in the form of physical hard copy and others as digital documentation. If someone came to me with a question, I knew I had the answers somewhere, but had no way to get that information quickly. Like most people, I was trying to rely on my memory to help me locate whatever piece of data I needed. I quickly learned that my brain could no longer be relied on to perform what I required of it. Perhaps it was an age thing, or maybe it was simply information overload. Whatever the reason, I found myself stressed and frustrated.

Then I saw a quote from Albert Einstein which said, "Never memorize anything you can look up." I had originally heard the quote paraphrased as something like this, "Why should I fill my brain with useless information that I can look up in five minutes?" I figured if anyone had a handle on how to use his brain to achieve the best results, it was my man Albert. For years I had another Einstein quote hanging on the wall which read, "Imagination is more important than knowledge."

Suddenly I realized my problem. I was cluttering my brain with useless data that, if organized properly, I could look up in a few minutes, or better yet, a few seconds. This would not only free my brain for more creative endeavors, but it would also relieve some of the stress I was feeling. The question was, how do I accomplish this? I struggled with this for many years trying different methods of organization. Some worked well, others not so much.

I had to find a way to get my life organized and be able to lay my finger on the information I needed at a moment's notice. Now that might sound simple, and it should be. But when you are working with thousands of documents in hundreds of subdirectories, each one containing specific information for a specific situation, things get complicated very quickly. I realized I had to come up with a better way to operate, or I was in real danger of failing. (Not a good thing when you rely on money to feed your family – like everyone else in the world.)

So, I came up with a system for using Microsoft Word to help me get my act together. Using MS Word and hyperlinks, I came up with a way not only to organize my professional life, but my personal life as well. The term hyperlink might sound scary and complicated to someone not computer savvy, but believe me, it's not. In this book I go into detailed explanations of how to create a personal network of documents that you will be able to use to make your life organized and much easier.

Let me state right off the bat, that I am in no way a computer wizard, nor am I a Microsoft Office guru. Like most users of the product, I know what I need to know to get by and basically know enough to make me dangerous. (This document, as you will see, is me being dangerous.) What I'll show you in this book is pretty much basic MS Word techniques, nothing fancy at all. In fact, if you are a computer wizard, you will probably laugh at my Link-Tuit system and say, "Any computer novice knows this crap, what are you trying to pull?"

What I've learned through the years is that the statement above is true. A great many people do know a lot of what I'm going to show in this book, but very few had chosen to use these features in the way I'm using them. It's sort of like a recipe where each of the ingredients are commonly known to anyone who has ever cooked; however, very few cooks have figured out how to use the ingredients in the combination to make a particular dish. It's like when you see something that is basically simple and you say, "Why didn't I think of that?" The reason you didn't is because, like most of us, you are too busy being the hamster on the exercise wheel.

I know this to be true because over the years, I have shown many people a lot smarter than I am how to use this system. And in almost every case, they said something like, "I like this. Why the heck didn't I think of that?" Sound familiar? For the record, this system didn't have the official name Link-Tuit until I decided to write this book. I figured it needed something catchy to attract some attention. In that regard, I beg your indulgence.

The fact is the name is unimportant. A rose by any other name… yadda, yadda, yadda. What is important is that as you read this book, you remember several things. First, I go into great and often what might seem like unnecessary detail when explaining a process, especially in the beginning. When I personally do any of these particular steps, they might only take me a few seconds whereas it may initially take several minutes for you and may even seem like a complete waste of time. But trust me, this system has pulled my bacon (yum, bacon) from the fire more times than I can tell you.

Continuing the food analogies, before you get into the meat and potatoes of this book, I want to point out a few assumptions I have necessarily made. If you don't fit into these assumptions, you may want to brush up a bit before proceeding.

I am assuming the reader has a general understanding of Microsoft Word. This book was written using Microsoft Word for Office 365. The techniques used in this book will work with older versions of Word and Office as well. The screens might look slightly different on the older versions, but the logic is the same.

I am also assuming you have a basic familiarity with computers and basic techniques such as creating a new file, left mouse clicking, right mouse clicking, scrolling, opening and closing files, saving files, copying and pasting both files as well as photos and text, and inserting page breaks. Again, you may want to make sure you can do these things before proceeding.

If you are a Microsoft expert or computer wizard, this document will still help you, but I will be honest, you may find it frustrating at times and over simplified. But hey, if you already knew how to do this, then how come you didn't come up with this system and write your own book, smarty pants? Just kidding. Geeze lighten up for Pete's sake.

There is another caveat I'd like to mention. Depending upon your personality, you may find this entire book a frustrating waste of time. I know that sounds harsh and not the sort of thing an author should be telling you at the start of his book, but I'm just being honest here. The system I outline in this book is geared to those of us in the technical world who are required to come up with answers. It has worked for me for many decades. It has saved me countless hours of searching and researching. My professional philosophy has been to only do things once, and then document it so I don't have to figure it out all over again. Sounds logical, right? But believe me, I know there are some of you out there with "that certain personality" that will think all of this is a complete waste of time.

That type of person is usually the person in charge, the one who is asking people like us to come up with the answers. They tend to be overwhelmed and "don't have time" to bother with such menial tasks. That's fine. That's why they pay you the big bucks. But for peons like us who must be relied upon to provide those answers, the Link-Tuit system is priceless. Again, it may take a few minutes longer in the beginning, but it will save you countless hours down the road.

If you've ever said, "Yeah, I have that information somewhere, I just have to put my finger on it," then Link-Tuit is the system for you because you can literally put your finger on it with the simple click of a mouse button on a hyperlink.

Believe me, this works. It has worked for me for over two decades and the more I use it, the more tricks and tips I come up with to make it work even better. Early in my career before PCs and the Internet (yeah, I'm that old) I had two four-foot by five-foot bookshelves filled with technical manuals; that was my reference library. Then computers arrived, and eventually so did digital manuals. Slowly, the books began to disappear from the shelves and updated versions reappeared on my computer. But organization was still a problem. Once I developed Link-Tuit, that problem went away. Now, I have everything I need at my fingertips, on a tiny two gigabyte thumb drive. Everything that I would have had to search for in volumes and volumes of documents, now resides on that single thumb drive (which by the way I back up every night — that's a good practice). And thanks to Link-Tuit, I can retrieve that information in a fraction of the time it formerly took to do so.

Whether you are an engineer, an accountant, a lawyer, a doctor, an automotive repair man, a plumber or any profession that requires you to have quick access to documentation Link-Tuit is for you. Suppose you don't need Link-Tuit in your professional life, but you're an artist, a writer, a musician or perhaps all three-in-one, Link-Tuit is the perfect way for you to organize your varied activities for quick access to information. The uses are endless.

So, without any further ado, let's get this Link-Tuit training underway.

←

Chapter 1

Setting Up MS Word

I'll keep this section very simple. You can use MS Word as is, right out of the box. But I like to make a few subtle changes to make my life easier. There are basically three things I recommend you set in MS Word before proceeding. They are all optional, but I have found they will save you a lot of grief down the road.

The first one is the most important of the three. It is changing a setting to make using hyperlinks much easier. You see, the default setting concerning hyperlinks is to press down the **Ctrl** key combined with the mouse click when selecting a hyperlink; however, I prefer to simply **left-mouse click** a hyperlink and not have the hassle of having to press another key.

To do this, click on the **File** tab and then scroll down and click **Options.**

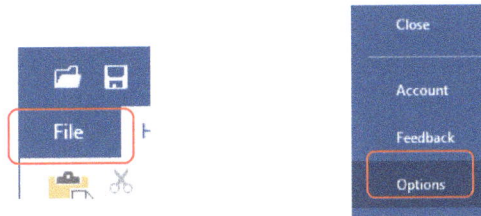

The **Word Options** window will appear with the **General Option** highlighted. Select the **Advanced Option**.

You will see the **Use CTRL + Click to follow hyperlink** option checked.

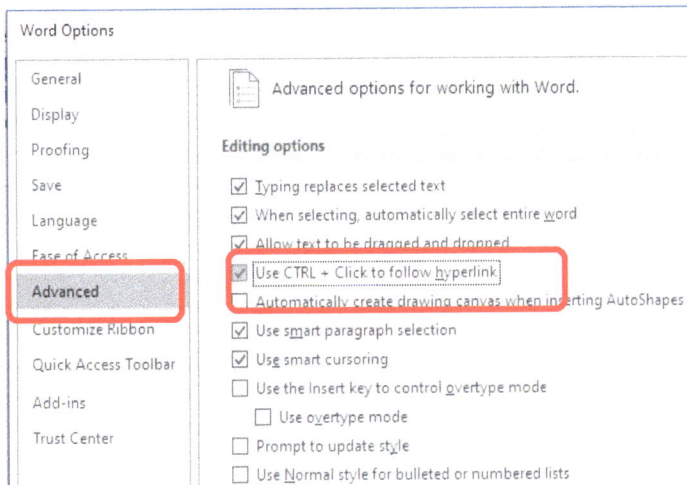

Uncheck the option so that it will not be necessary to use the **CTRL** key in conjunction with **clicking** the hyperlink.

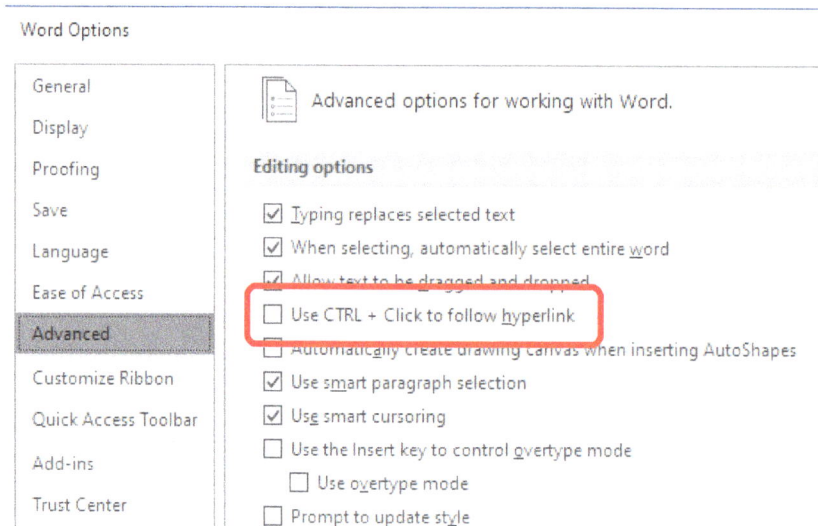

Word Options

General	Advanced options for working with Word.
Display	
Proofing	**Editing options**
Save	☑ Typing replaces selected text
Language	☑ When selecting, automatically select entire word
Ease of Access	☑ Allow text to be dragged and dropped
Advanced	☐ Use CTRL + Click to follow hyperlink
Customize Ribbon	☐ Automatically create drawing canvas when inserting AutoShapes
Quick Access Toolbar	☑ Use smart paragraph selection
Add-ins	☑ Use smart cursoring
Trust Center	☐ Use the Insert key to control overtype mode
	☐ Use overtype mode
	☐ Prompt to update style

The second feature to change is adding two icons to my **Quick Access Toolbar**. These icons are **Insert a Bookmark** and **Add a Hyperlink**.

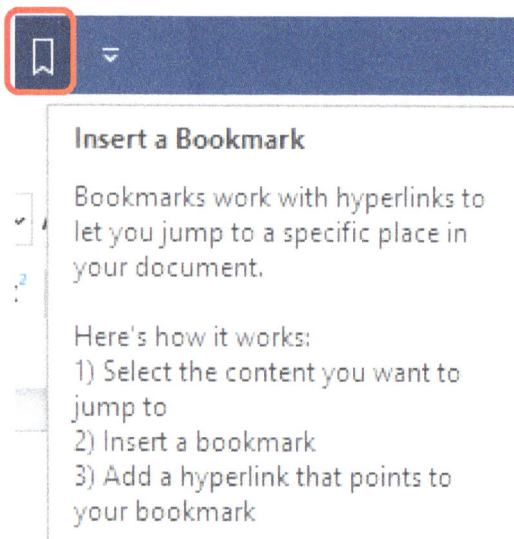

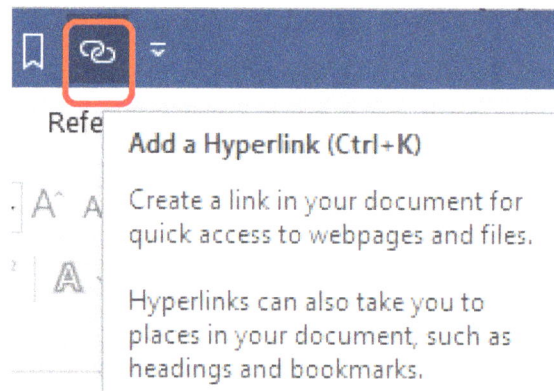

Insert a Bookmark

Bookmarks work with hyperlinks to let you jump to a specific place in your document.

Here's how it works:
1) Select the content you want to jump to
2) Insert a bookmark
3) Add a hyperlink that points to your bookmark

Add a Hyperlink (Ctrl+K)

Create a link in your document for quick access to webpages and files.

Hyperlinks can also take you to places in your document, such as headings and bookmarks.

Having these icons in your **Quick Access Toolbar** will save you a lot of time, especially the more involved you get with using this method of organization.

To put these icons onto your **Quick Access Toolbar**, right click on the **Quick Access Toolbar,** then select **Customize Quick Access Toolbar**.

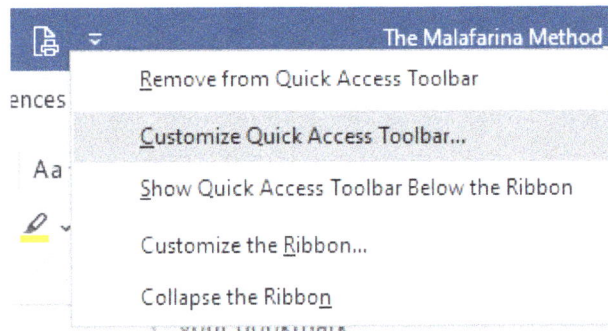

The **Word Options** window will appear with a list of all the options you currently have active on your **Quick Access Toolbar** as well as a list of other options you can add. We are going to add the **Add a Hyperlink** option first.

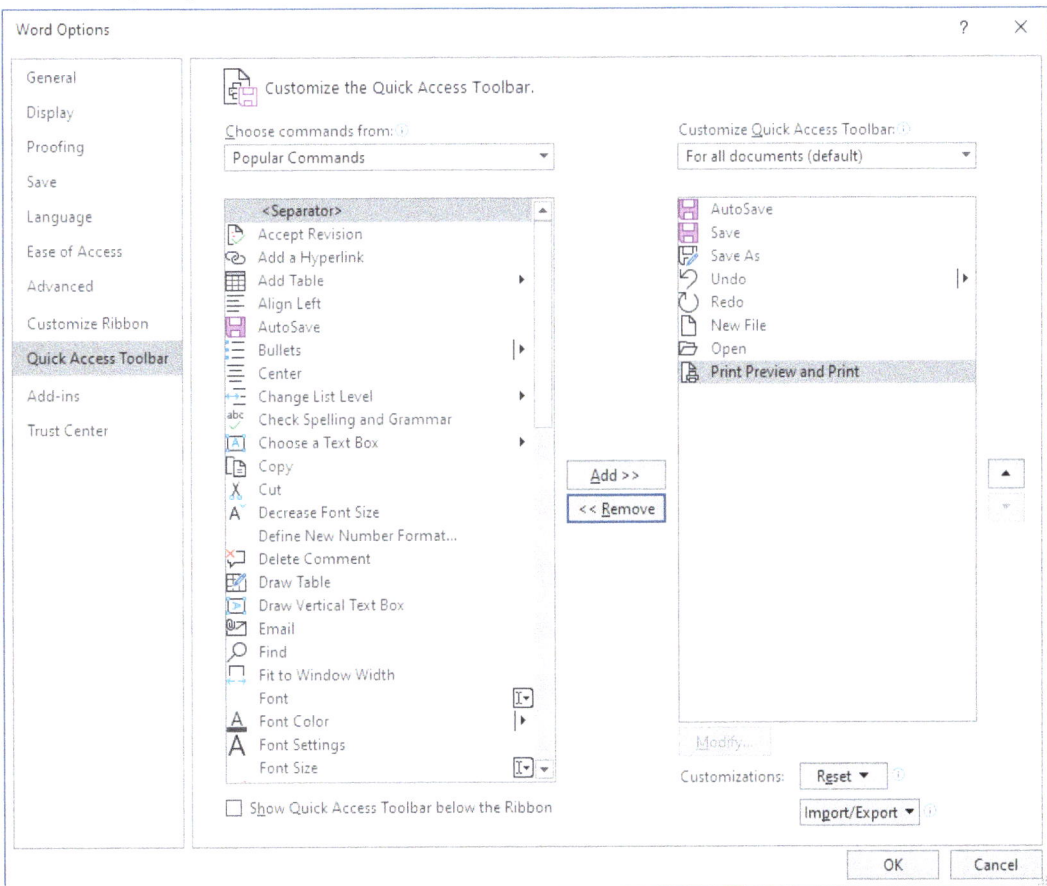

You will see the current list of options is set for **Popular Commands**. You can change this by clicking the down arrow next to the words **Popular Commands**.

As you can see, there are a lot of options available. For now, we are going to stick with **Popular Commands**.

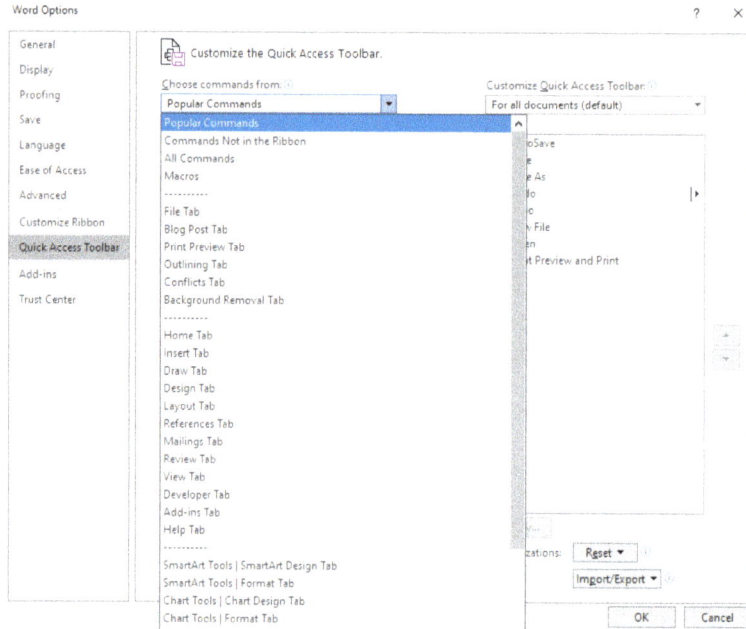

As you can see below **Add a Hyperlink** is the second option available under **Popular Commands**.

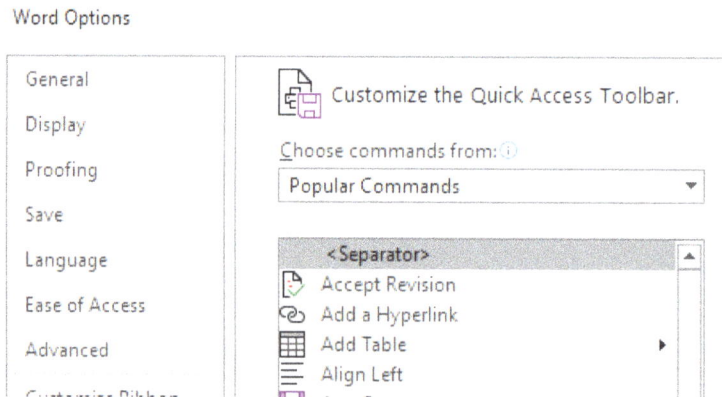

Click on **Add a Hyperlink,** then click on the **Add >>** button.

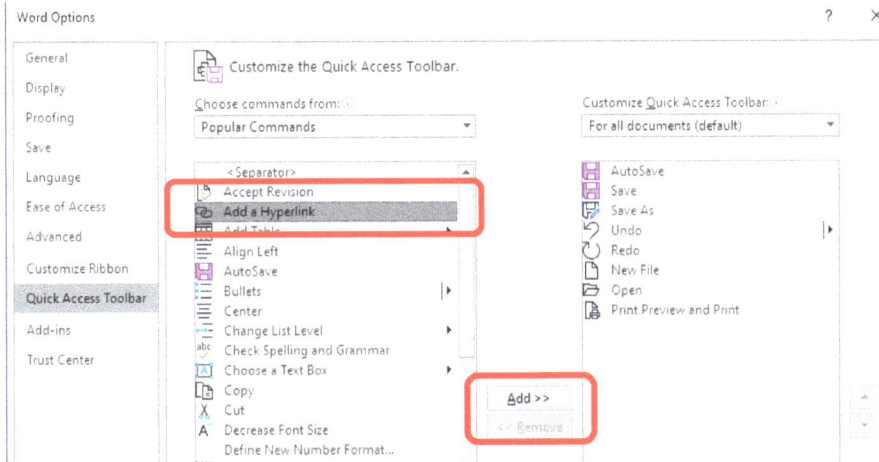

This will add the **Add a Hyperlink** option to your **Quick Access Toolbar** at the bottom of the list. Click **OK** to accept this.

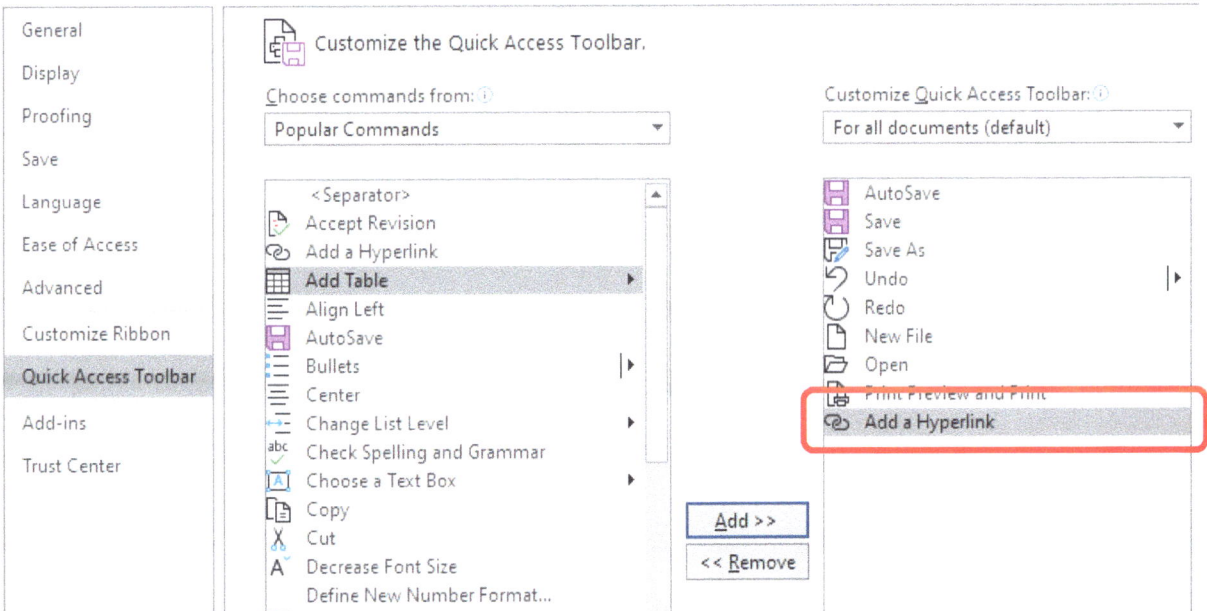

Now let's find and add the **Insert a Bookmark** icon to our **Quick Access Toolbar.**

This one is a little trickier because as you scroll down through your alphabetized **Popular Commands** list, you won't find it there.

Hummm, what to do, what to do??

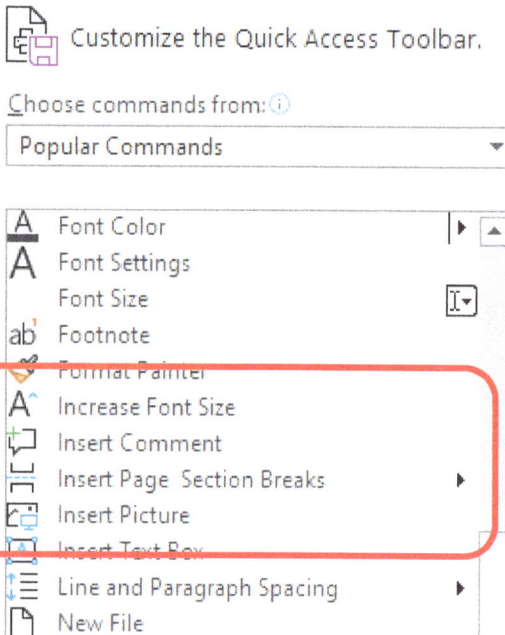
Customize the Quick Access Toolbar.

Choose commands from: ⓘ

Popular Commands

A — Font Color
A — Font Settings
Font Size
ab¹ — Footnote
Format Painter
A^ — Increase Font Size
Insert Comment
Insert Page Section Breaks
Insert Picture
Insert Text Box
Line and Paragraph Spacing
New File

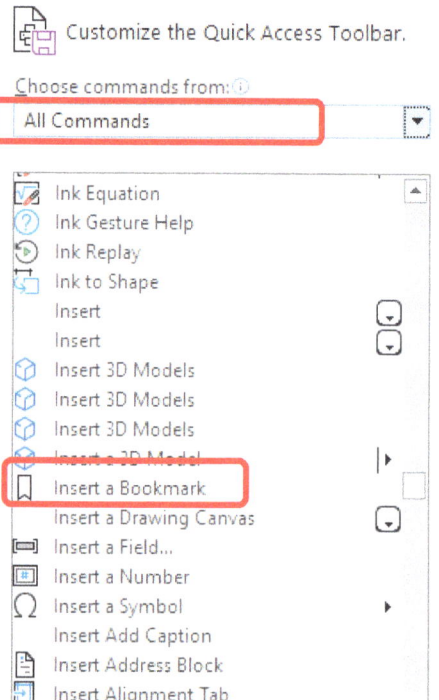
Customize the Quick Access Toolbar.

Choose commands from: ⓘ

All Commands

Ink Equation
Ink Gesture Help
Ink Replay
Ink to Shape
Insert
Insert
Insert 3D Models
Insert 3D Models
Insert 3D Models
Insert a 3D Model
Insert a Bookmark
Insert a Drawing Canvas
Insert a Field...
Insert a Number
Insert a Symbol
Insert Add Caption
Insert Address Block
Insert Alignment Tab

If you didn't know the exact name of the option you wanted, you could spend a lot of time looking for it. (I know because I have.) We're lucky; we know it is called **Insert a Bookmark**.

All we have to do is change our option choice from **Popular Commands** to **All Commands**, then scroll down until we get to the **Insert a Bookmark** option.

Like before, we'll first select the option then select **Add** to move it over to the **Quick Access Toolbar** then **OK** to accept it.

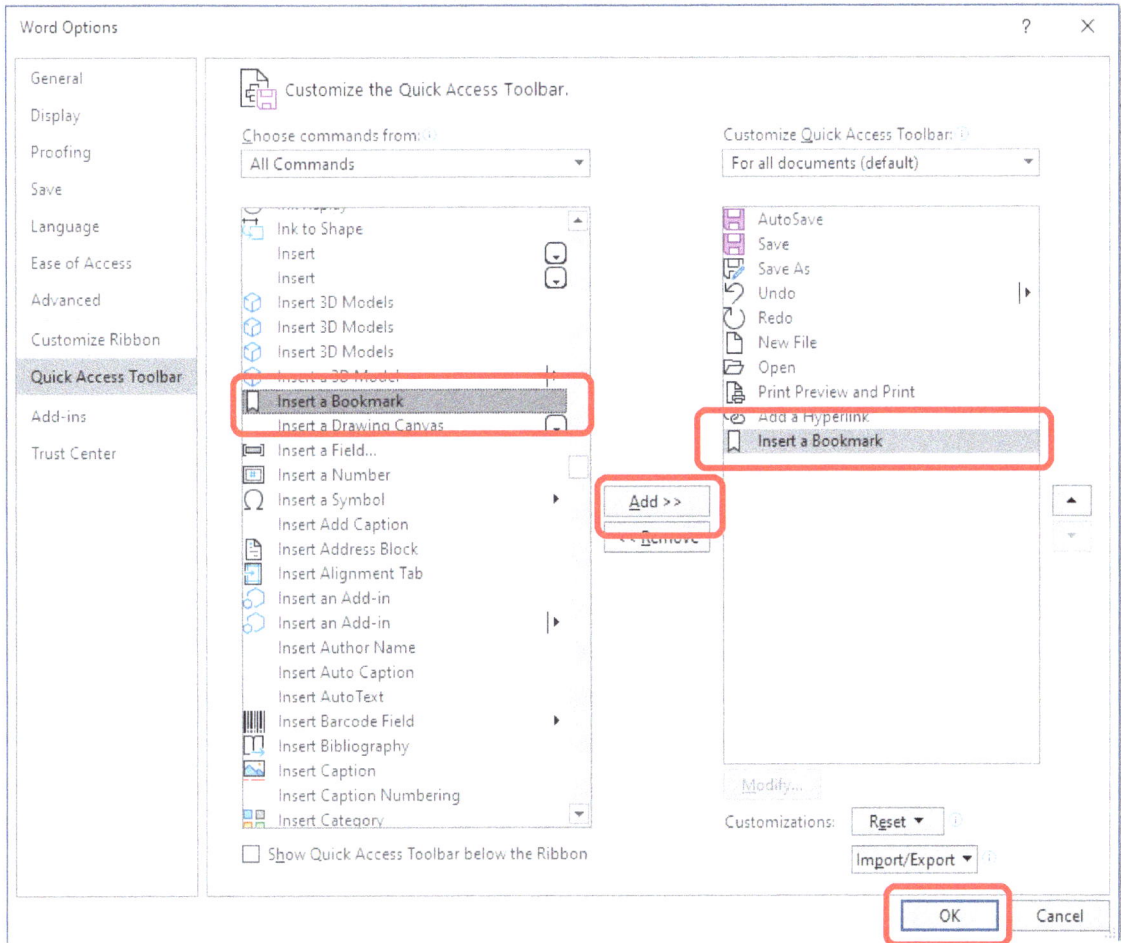

There you go. You've added the two options to your **Quick Access Toolbar**.

But here is something you might want to consider for your personal preference.

As you can see, the order in which the options are listed above is the same order in which they will appear on the **Quick Access Toolbar** shown below.

If you are fine with the order, don't change it. But I like to have the **Insert a Bookmark** before the **Add a Hyperlink,** and I like my **Print Preview and Print** icon at the end of the list. Yeah, I know, it's weird, but so am I.

Anyway, to move your icons around, while you have your list displayed, select the desired icon and then click the **UP** or **DOWN** side arrows to move them to the location you prefer, then click **OK**.

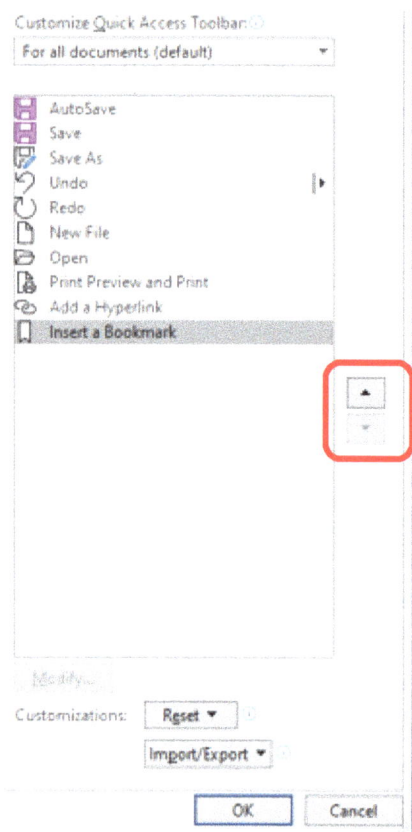

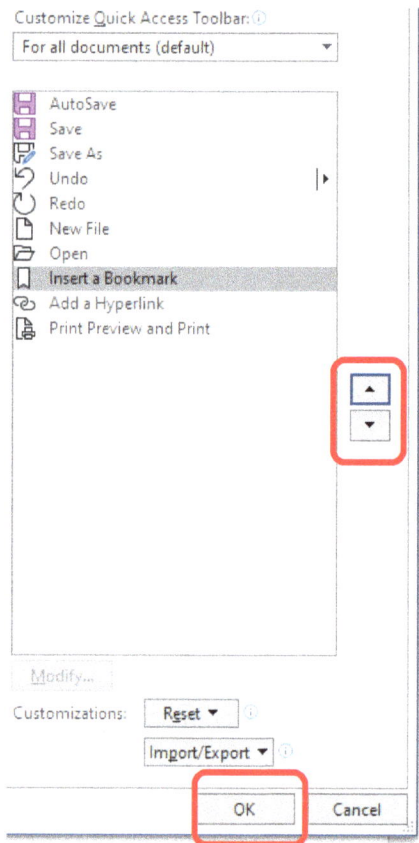

Then like magic, they appear in the order I prefer them. Ah, now all is right with the world

If you decide to skip this option, you are on your own. You can look up how to access **Insert a Bookmark** and **Add a Hyperlink** some other way in Word.

Ok, now on to the next option. This one is to set a default font for your documents. Perhaps the default fonts are not what you like, so rather than changing them every time you create a new document, you can change them once, set them, and forget them. For example, I like Arial font and size 12. I'm not married to the font and have changed it several times during my career. Heck, I might change my preference tomorrow. Anyway, here is how you change it.

Under the **Home** tab, select the arrow next to the word **Font** or press **Ctrl +D**.

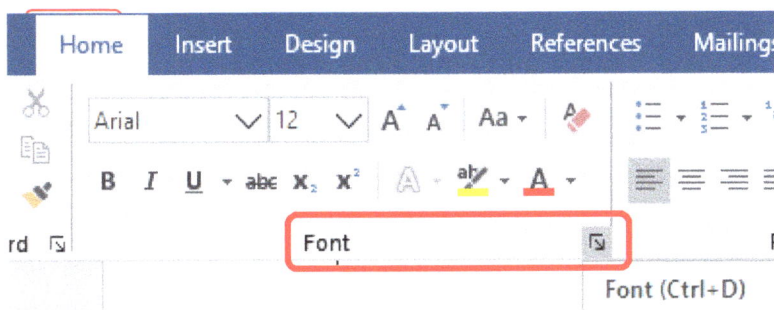

This will bring up the **Font** option menu where you can select your desired font.

Once you have set the font style and the size you like, select **Set As Default,** then select **OK** to make it your default font every time you create a document.

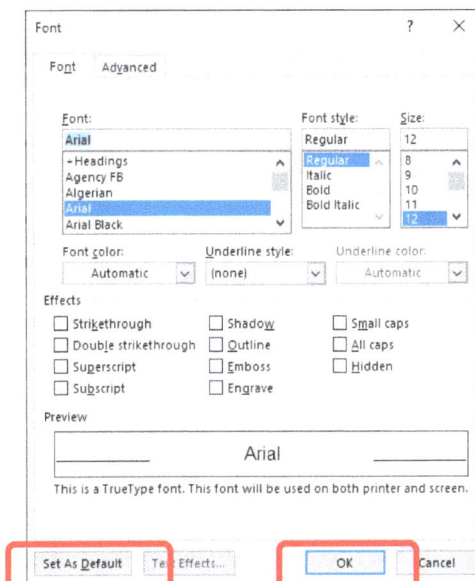

9

You will be prompted with the message below to allow you to decide if you want to make the change for **This document only** or **All future documents based on the Normal startup template**.

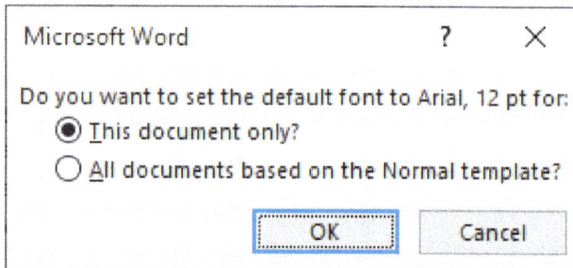

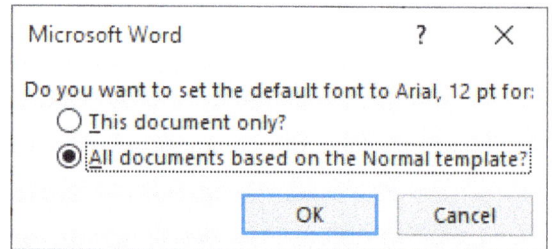

Microsoft Word	?	✕

Do you want to set the default font to Arial, 12 pt for:
- ⦿ T̲his document only?
- ◯ A̲ll documents based on the Normal template?

    [OK   ]   [Cancel   ]

Microsoft Word	?	✕

Do you want to set the default font to Arial, 12 pt for:
- ◯ T̲his document only?
- ⦿ A̲ll documents based on the Normal template?

    [OK   ]   [Cancel   ]

If you choose **All documents based on the Normal template**, then all future new documents will use your default font when created.

←

Chapter 2

A Simple Hyperlinked Document

One more thing. For this training session, create a subdirectory called Link-Tuit on your hard drive which we will use from this point onward.

Something to keep in mind about hyperlinks…

If you have files stored in a subdirectory or subdirectories and you either move them or rename them, any existing hyperlinks will be broken and will no longer work.

So, care must be taken when naming your files and creating subdirectories. If you are the only one using these documents and directories, it is usually not much of a problem. But if you are sharing your documents on a network, you must maintain strict control or risk having to re-establish links.

This is not necessarily a big deal, but depending upon the complexity of your document network, it could quickly become one.

Ok. Let's get this party started. As with any training I do, I like to start with something as simple as possible.

We're going to create a new Word document with a table of contents that hyperlinks to a variety of places within the same document. It will also have the ability to hyperlink back to the table of contents. I'll encourage you to save this document as a sort of template to use to save you time in the future until you get used to using this technique.

First let's start a new Word document.

Select **File**, then select **Blank document**.

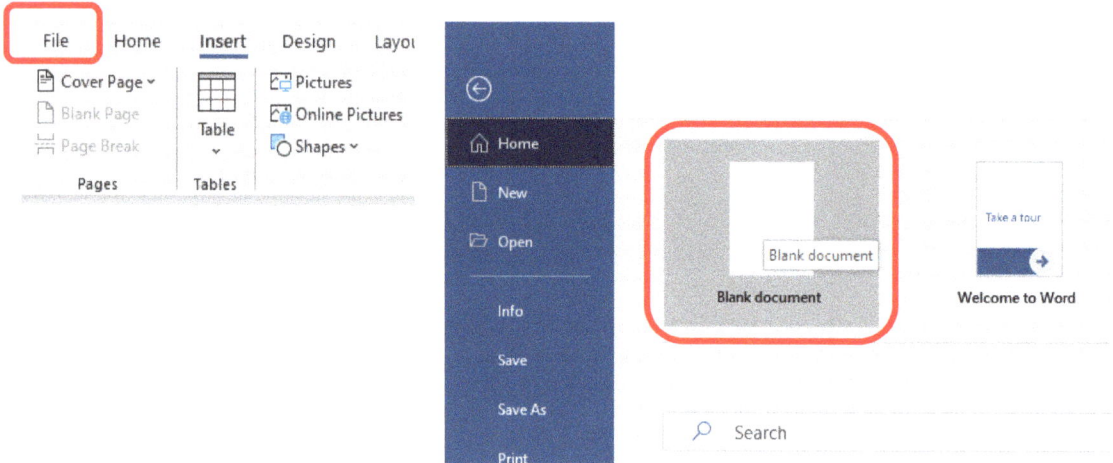

This will create a new blank document.

If you followed the instructions in the first chapter to set a default font of your choice, the new document should automatically be using that font. As you may remember, I set mine to Arial font, 12 pt. size.

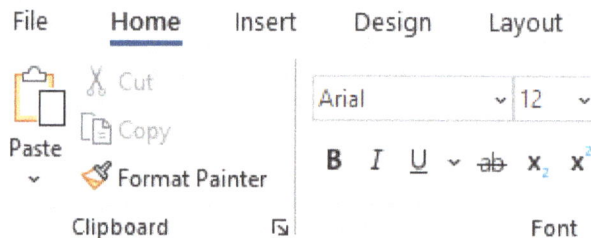

Save the new file in the current subdirectory as **Startup File**.

Now type the words **Table Of Contents** on the first line of the document as shown below.

Table Of Contents

For now, we won't get fancy, but at some point, you may want to change the font size, color, and style to give your document an appearance that works for you.

Under **Table Of Contents,** type **Section 1** then **Section 2** then **Section 3** as shown below.

Table Of Contents

Section 1

Section 2

Section 3

Now you have your simple table of contents.

At this point, we're going to add our bookmarks. We don't have to do this now; we could wait until later. In fact, I often do wait until later, but since we are on this section, let's do this so we can move on with the rest of the demonstration.

Word will not let you start a bookmark with a number.
It also will not allow spaces or special characters such as dashes or other such characters. It will, however, allow the underscore character.

I'll show you what I mean. Place your curser in front of the line reading Section 1. Then select the **Insert a Bookmark** icon.

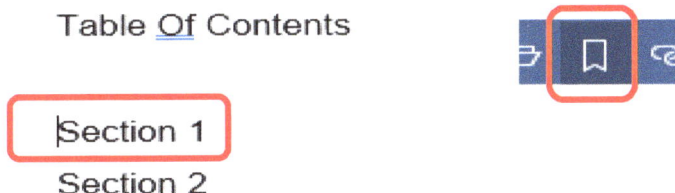

Table Of Contents

Section 1
Section 2

The bookmark window will appear for you to enter the name of your bookmark.

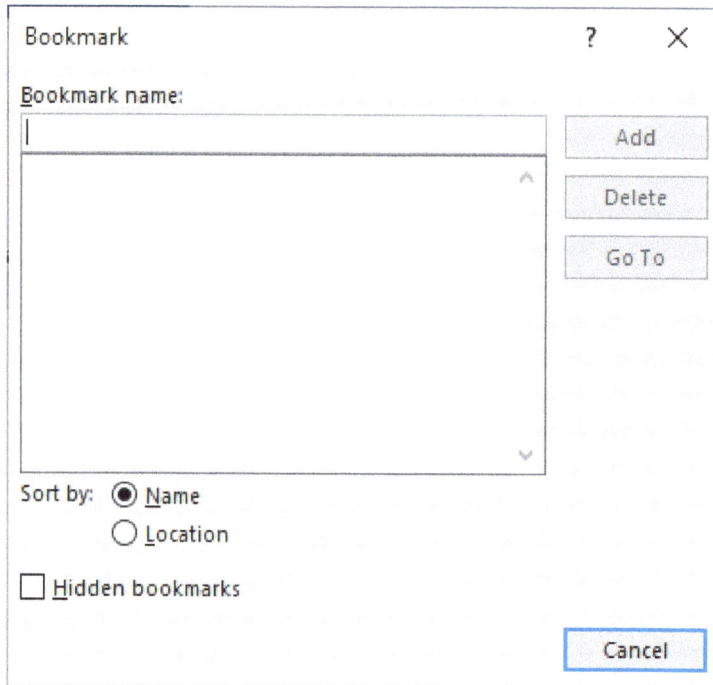

Let's do an experiment. Type in the word **Section**. You will see the **Add** button highlight. This tells us the word we typed was acceptable for a bookmark.

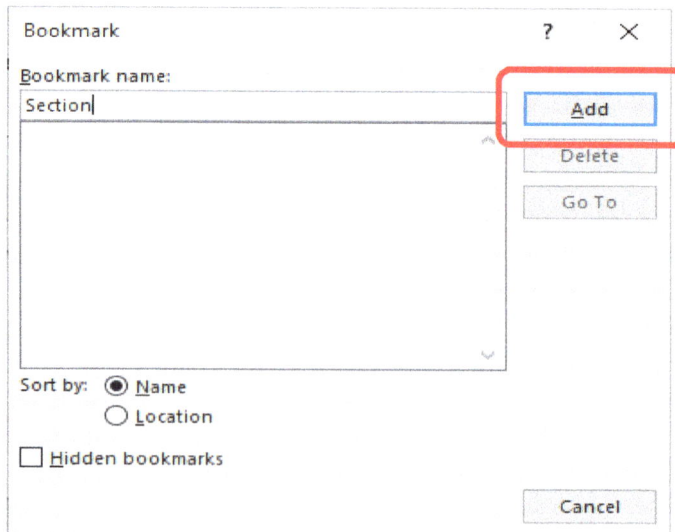

Now backspace to delete all the characters and type **1Section.**

Bookmark	? ✕
Bookmark name:	
1Section|	Add
	Delete
	Go To
Sort by: ● Name	
○ Location	
☐ Hidden bookmarks	
	Cancel

You will see that the **ADD** button does not highlight. This tells you the name you chose for a bookmark is not good. Had you been watching the **ADD** button as you typed, you would have seen its highlighting disappear as soon as the number 1 was typed.

Backspace again to eliminate the letters, and then slowly type **Section-1**, keeping your eye on the **ADD** button. As you type, you will see the button stays highlighted until it sees the dash (-).

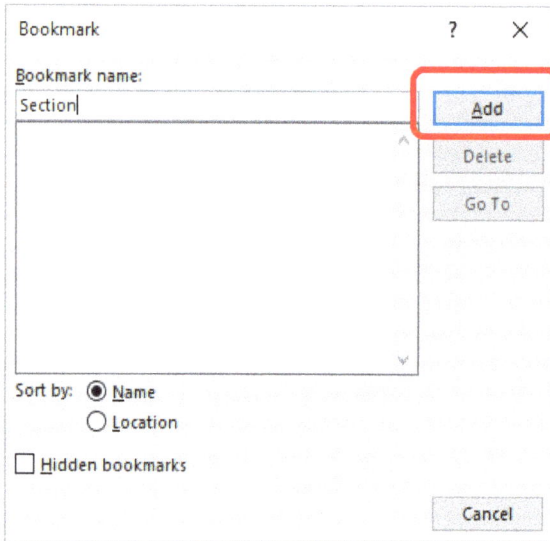

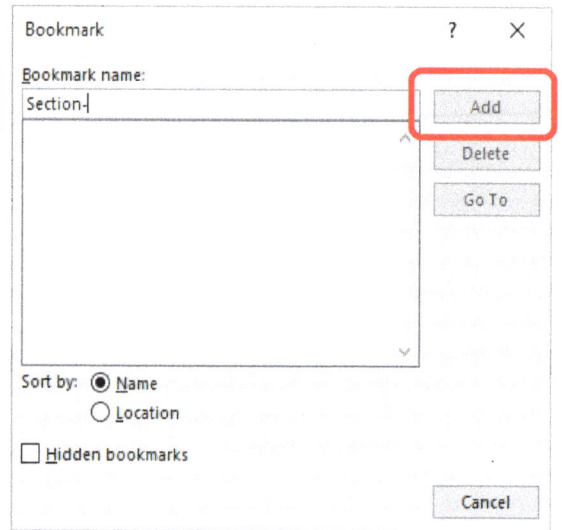

That's because it doesn't like the dash. The same thing would happen with spaces. It will accept the underscore character if you want to space words.

Backspace to remove all the letters and type **Section_1_TOC**.

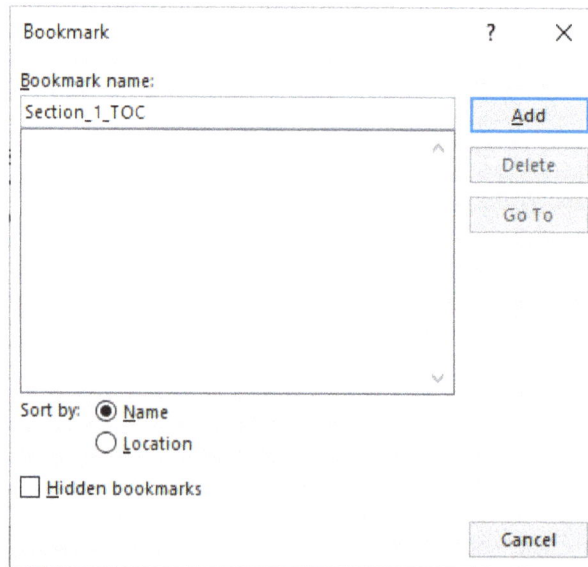

You'll see that all the characters are acceptable. You'll also notice I added the capital letters **TOC** at the end of the line. This is my own personal preference. I have adapted the standard convention of following all of my names in my **Table of Contents** with the letters **TOC**. This allows me to use the same name without the **TOC** to identify the section I want to hyperlink to, which we will get to shortly.

For now, just humor me and stick with my naming preference. Click the **ADD** button to add the bookmark to the place in front of the line labeled **Section 1**. Then do the same thing for **Section 2** with the description **Section_2_TOC** and then **Section 3** with the description **Section_3_TOC**.

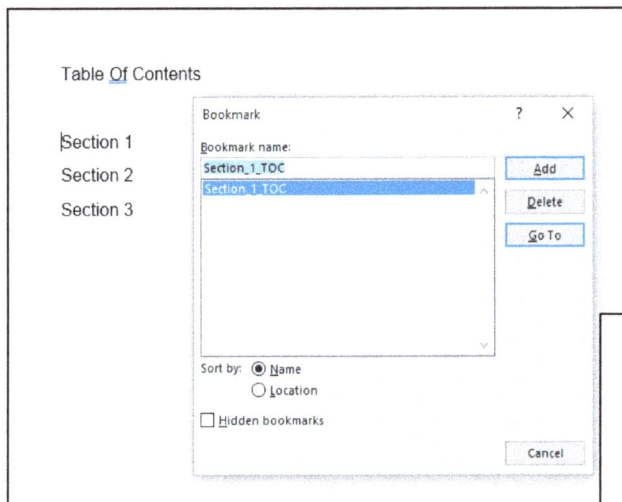

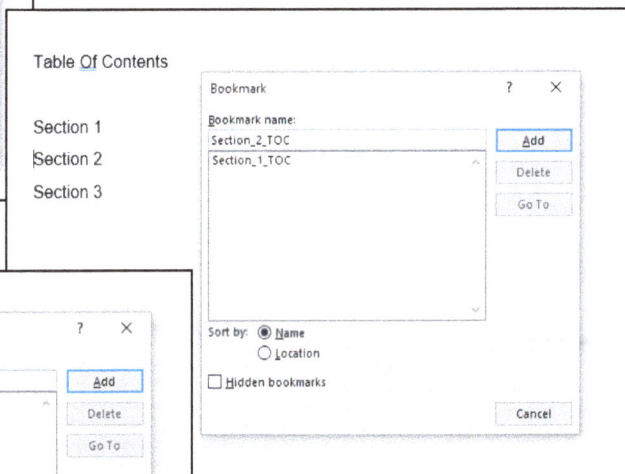

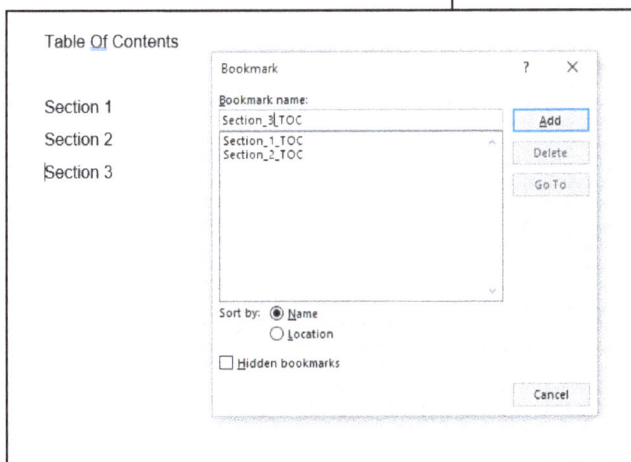

Now be sure to **SAVE** the document. And do so often.

What we have done so far is create a small table of contents for this document and assigned bookmarks to each of our table of contents items. These bookmarks will become critical for us when it comes to hyperlinking around the document.

This all may seem like a lot of work, but trust me, once you get the hang of this it goes really quickly and the limited amount of time it costs you to create these hyperlinked documents will save you tons of time down the road.

Now we are going to create pages that represent the various topics covered within our document. We'll create one for **Section 1**, then **Section 2,** then **Section 3**. I will go into detail about the process for **Section 1** and then let you on your own to create the pages for **Section 2** and **Section 3** as they are created identically to **Section 1**.

Put a few blank lines under the words **Section 3** in your table of contents to allow space for future table items, then insert a **Page Break** to start a new page.

Table Of Contents

Section 1

Section 2

Section 3

|

Now on this new page, type the items shown to the right:

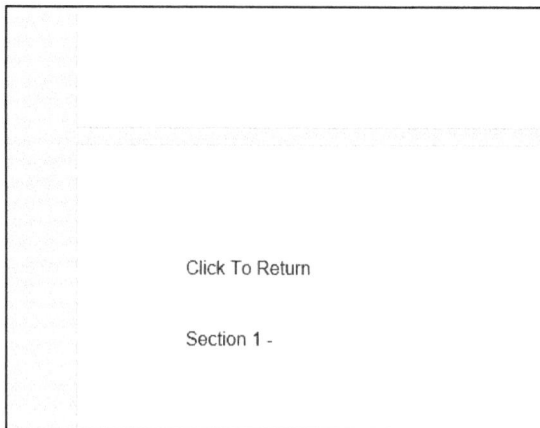

Click To Return

Section 1 -

The words **Click To Return** are what I like to use so that the users of the document (other than me) will know that if they click that line they will return to the **Table of Contents**.

If you prefer, you could simply type **Return** or **Go Home** or any word or phrase you choose.

Just in case you were wondering, you could also use a symbol or picture in place of these words because hyperlinks work for both. You probably didn't notice, but in this document, which is also hyperlinked in MS Word or PDF format, I used a back-arrow icon for my hyperlink to allow me to navigate easily from chapter to chapter. That being said, I only used that in this document, as it is easily overlooked by the casual reader and basically serves me for my purposes. In my other documents, I like to use **Click To Return**. Regardless of what method you use, I recommend finding something you like and sticking with it so you can standardize.

If you do choose to use a symbol for your hyperlink rather than a word or phrase, you can add a screen tip to your symbol so whenever someone moves the cursor over the symbol, it will tell them the symbol is used to return them to the Table of Contents.

To do this, right click the symbol and select the **Edit Link** (or **Edit Hyperlink**) option from the drop-down menu.

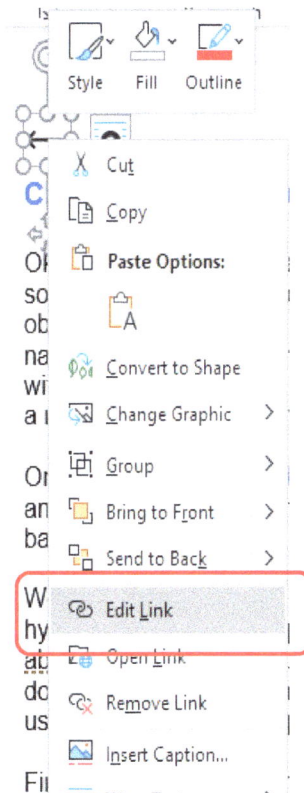

Then from the **Edit Hyperlink** window, select **ScreenTip** button.

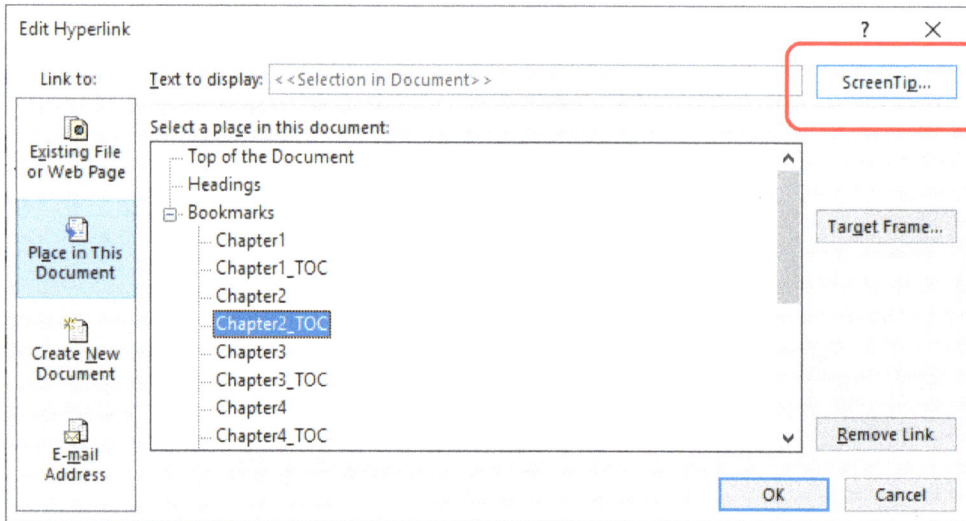

When the **Set Hyperlink Screen Tip** window appears, type in whatever you want your screen tip to say, for example, "**Return To Table Of Contents**."

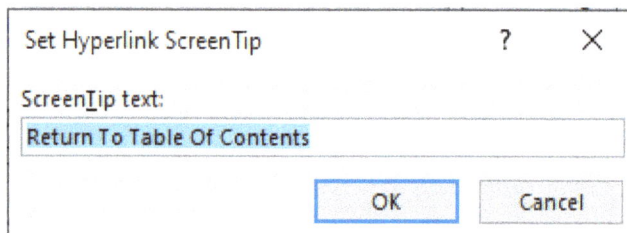

Then press **OK** to leave the **Set Hyperlink ScreenTip** window.

And press **OK** to leave the **Edit Hyperlink** window.

Whenever you hover your cursor over your hyperlinked symbol, you will see your screen tip appear.

Ok, so it's not all that miraculous, but I thought it was kind of a cool feature.

For the record, you can also do this with a typed return link such as my "Click To Return" hyperlink, but I think that would be sort of redundant.

Now, let's continue. Highlight the line on the page which reads **Section 1**, then select the **Insert a Bookmark** icon.

We are going to add another bookmark here so that when we put in our hyperlinks, the document knows what to look for.

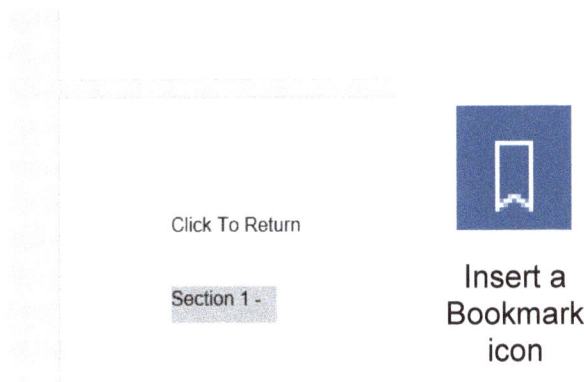

Click To Return

Section 1 -

Insert a
Bookmark
icon

When the **Bookmark** window appears, highlight the line reading **Section_1_TOC**; it will appear on the top line.

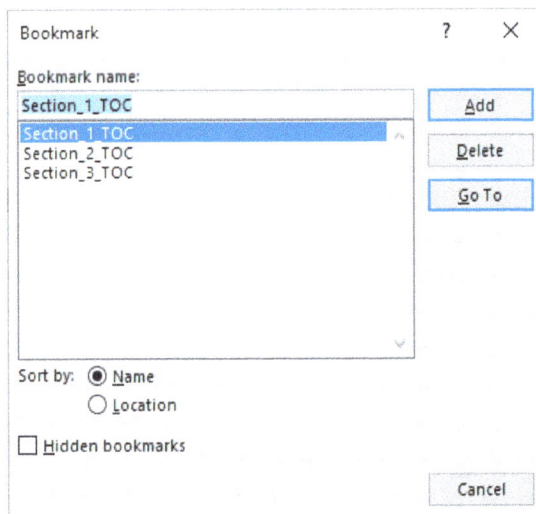

Bookmark	? ✕
Bookmark name:	
Section_1_TOC	Add
Section_1_TOC	Delete
Section_2_TOC	Go To
Section_3_TOC	

Sort by: ⦿ Name
○ Location

☐ Hidden bookmarks

Cancel

Remember before how I said I like to use the same naming convention for bookmarks in the section I will be hyperlinking to as the **Table Of Contents**?

Simply click on the **Bookmark name** field and backspace until the **_TOC** letters are gone, then select **ADD**.

This will create a bookmark at the title line of this page called **Section_1**.

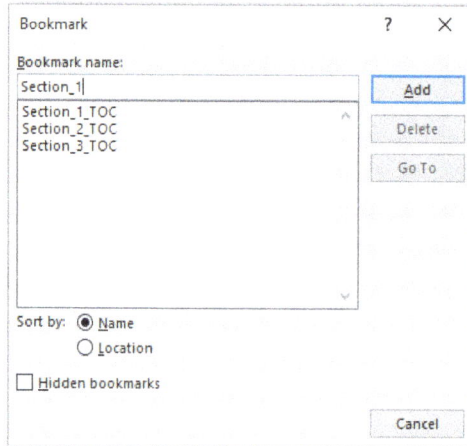

Now you have a page in your document with a bookmark called **Section_1** and a bookmark in your **Table Of Contents** called **Section_1_TOC**.

Now we can create hyperlinks that will allow us to bounce back and forth between sections of this document in the blink of an eye.

Highlight the first line on this page — the one that reads **Click To Return** — then select the **Add a Hyperlink** icon.

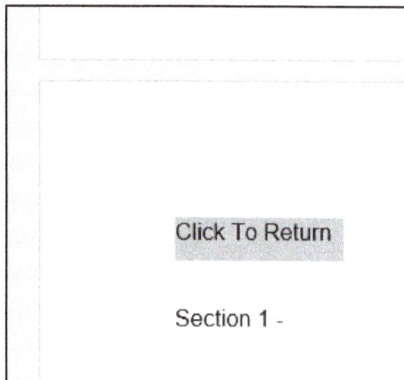

Add a Hyperlink icon

When the **Insert Hyperlink** window appears, you may see all the bookmarks you have created for this document. If not, be sure to select **Place in This Document** then Highlight **Section_1_TOC** and click **OK** because we want to hyperlink back to that place in our **Table Of Contents**.

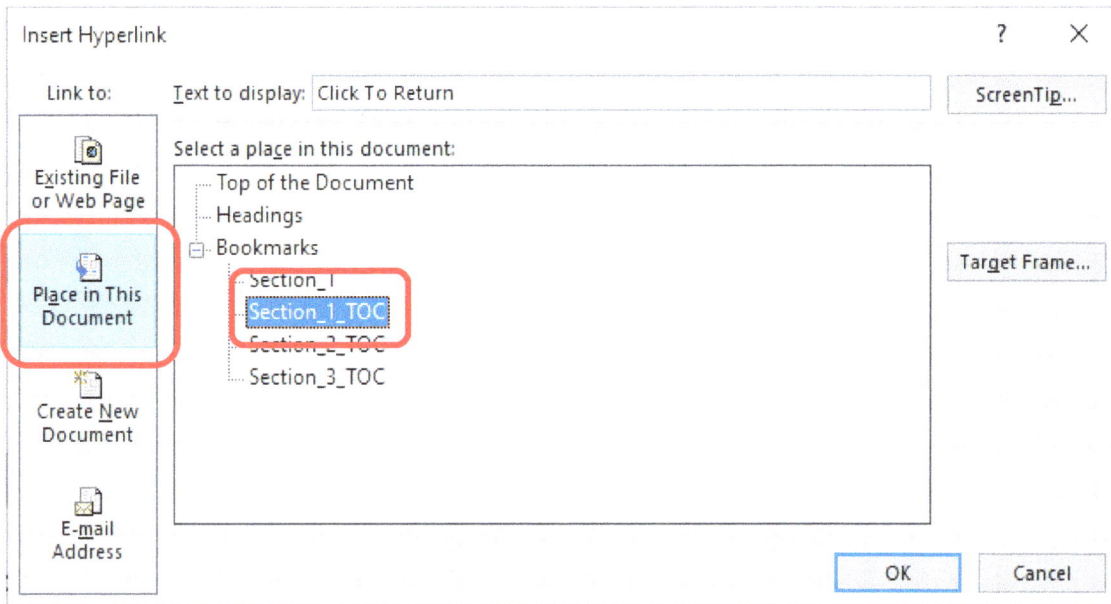

You will see the line change to reflect that it has become an active hyperlink. It will be blue and underlined.

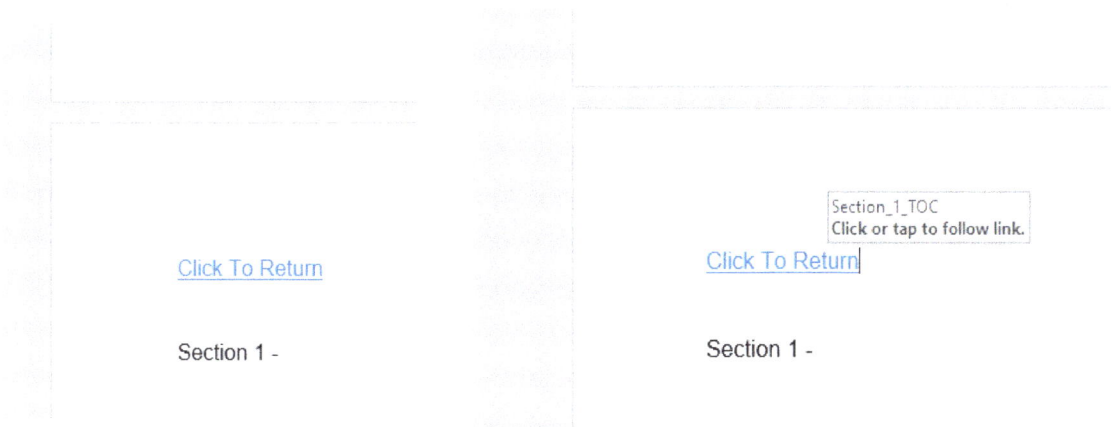

If you have changed the hyperlink setting as we discussed back in Chapter 1 and you run your cursor over the hyperlink, it should tell you to **Click or tap to follow link**. If you didn't change your setting it will ask you to press the combination of **Ctrl + Click.** I sure hope you changed it, because this is the last time, I plan on mentioning this.

Now click the line and see what happens.

That's right! Like magic, it took you back to the **Table of Contents** and placed your cursor right next to the line marked **Section 1**. Cool, huh?

Well, here is where it gets even cooler.

Select the line marked **Section 1**, and then select the **Add a Hyperlink** icon

When the **Insert Hyperlink** window appears, highlight the **Section_1** bookmark (remember that is what we used to identify the title on our page), then select **OK**.

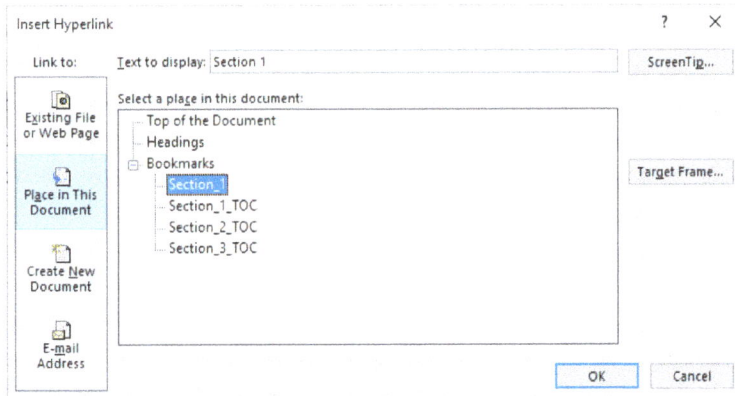

You have now created a hyperlink back to the page we created.

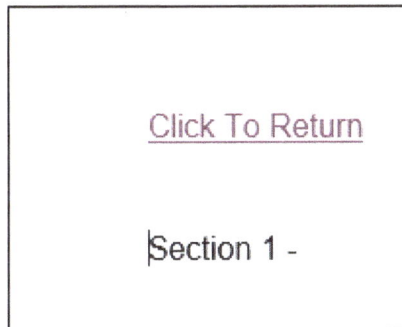

You will notice that the hyperlink has changed from blue to purple. This shows that you have clicked on the hyperlink.

When you eventually close and re-open the document it will return to blue until you click it again.

Now try something just for fun. Click the **Click to Return** again to go back to the **Table of Contents**, then return to this page. Pretty cool, right?

This may not be such a big deal when you have a two-page document, but what about when you have a 300 page document full of complex technical information or critical data that you need to access as quickly as possible?

Using Link-Tuit, you can be wherever you need to be in a second.

Ok, now it's your turn.

Using the instructions above, create two more pages below the current one (all separate pages with page breaks) for **Section 2** and **Section 3** and hyperlink them to their corresponding sections of the Table Of Contents.

Go ahead, I'll wait.

Humm hum hum hum (this is me waiting…)

…Ok, so you're back already. Cool.

Let me show you what mine looks like. I have some standards I like to use when I'm creating these documents, but you can use whatever you choose; after all, these are your notes and your information that you are compiling so they should look the way you want them to.

Here's my **Table Of Contents**
with all the hyperlinks in place and
active.

I like to use navy blue size 14 for
topic headings and use the default
blue for hyperlinks in my **Table Of
Contents**.

On my pages, I like to change the hyperlink which gets me back in bold, italicized
red. I use the same size 14 blue for my title and go back to black size 12 for content.
Hey Red, White and Blue. How American!

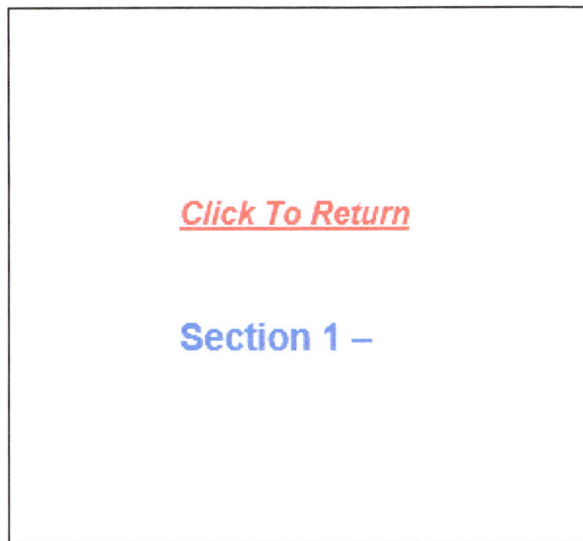

I realize the first few times you do this; it seems to take way too long. But believe
me, doing this entire three-page document with Table Of Contents, bookmarks,
hyperlinks, and formatting only took me about five minutes.

Again, this is about as simple as you can get. But as this book progresses, you will
see many other ways you can use Link-Tuit to organize your life. To be honest,
what you will learn from here on out is basically the same thing we have done so far
but expanded by situations I have encountered in my many years of using this
technique.

←

Chapter 3

Calling A Document From Another Document And Returning

So, what if you have a very complex collection of notes or have a variety of MS Word documents that you have stored in a variety of different subdirectories on your computer?

We all know what a hassle it can be bouncing around from subdirectory to subdirectory trying to find a file you know you have somewhere but can't seem to remember where.

Using Link-Tuit, you can create a document which you can use to hyperlink to the file and or directory you want with a few mouse clicks.

Let's first add some subdirectories to our original LinkTuit directory.

Create subdirectories under Link-Tuit directory called **Section 4**, **Section 5**, and **Section 6**.

> Link-Tuit >			
Name ∧	Date modified	Type	Size
Section 4	12/26/2019 4:10 PM	File folder	
Section 5	12/26/2019 2:17 PM	File folder	
Section 6	12/26/2019 2:17 PM	File folder	

Next, open your **Startup File**, (unless you still have it opened) and add three lines to the **Table Of Contents** — **Section 4**, **Section 5** and **Section 6**. Then **Insert a Bookmark** before each option.

Often, when I am going to call a document from another document, I will add the note (Separate DOC) so that I'm aware that this link will take me to a separate document that is not part of the current document. I don't want to get ahead of myself here, but I use the word DOC so I know it's a Word document I am linking to, and not an Excel file, a video, a PDF, or any other such item. We'll talk about these later.

Below is an example of how your **Startup File** will look:

Save the file (just a reminder in case you don't have autosave activated),

Now create a new Word document as shown below, and save it as **Section 4** in **Section 4** subdirectory.

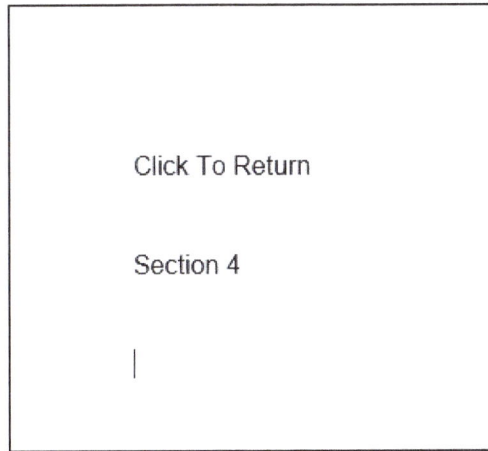

```
                  Click To Return


                  Section 4


                  |
```

ooks > Link-Tuit > Section 4

Name	Date modified	Type	Size
Section 4	12/26/2019 2:59 PM	Microsoft Word D...	12 KB

Now let's create a hyperlink on the line **Click To Return**, which will connect you back to the **Startup File** in the main directory.

Select the **Click To Return** line then select the **Add a Hyperlink** icon.

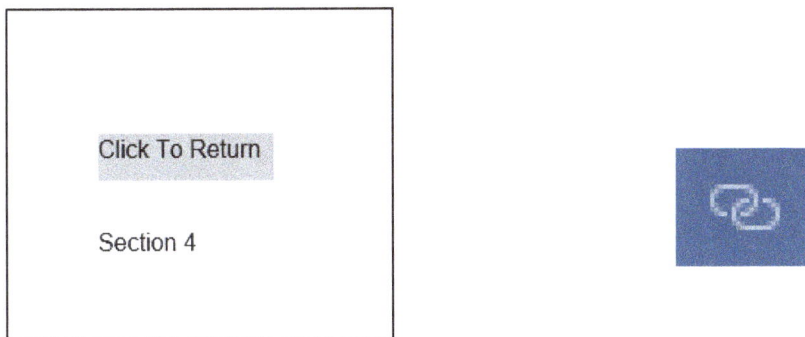

```
         Click To Return

         Section 4
```

The **Insert Hyperlink** window will appear.

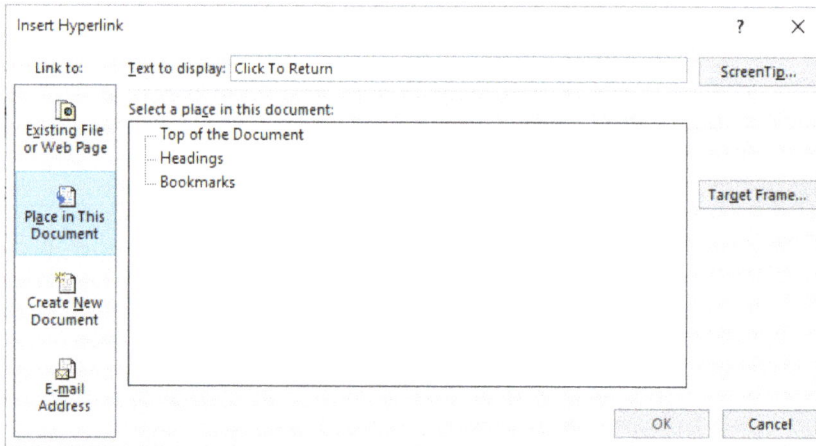

Since we are not looking for a bookmark within this document but in a different document, we must switch from **Place in This Document** to **Existing File or Web Page**.

It will show our current folder, but the document we want, our **Startup File**, is in the main directory, so we need do back up one folder level.

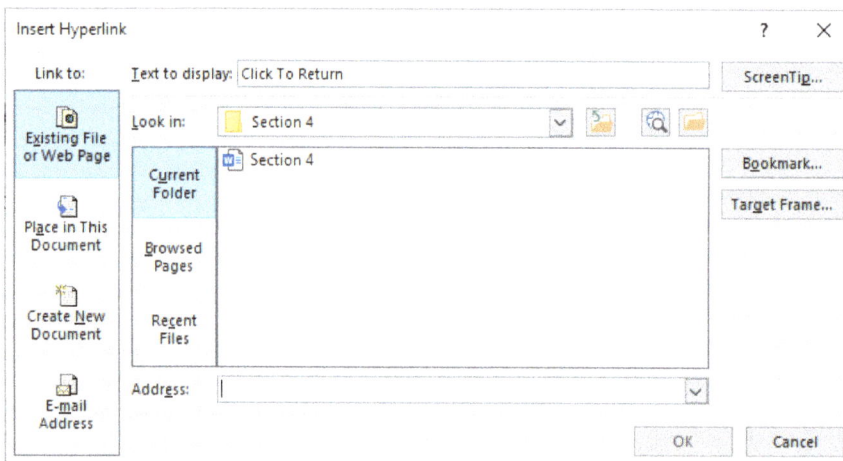

Select the **Up One Folder** icon to back up to the main directory.

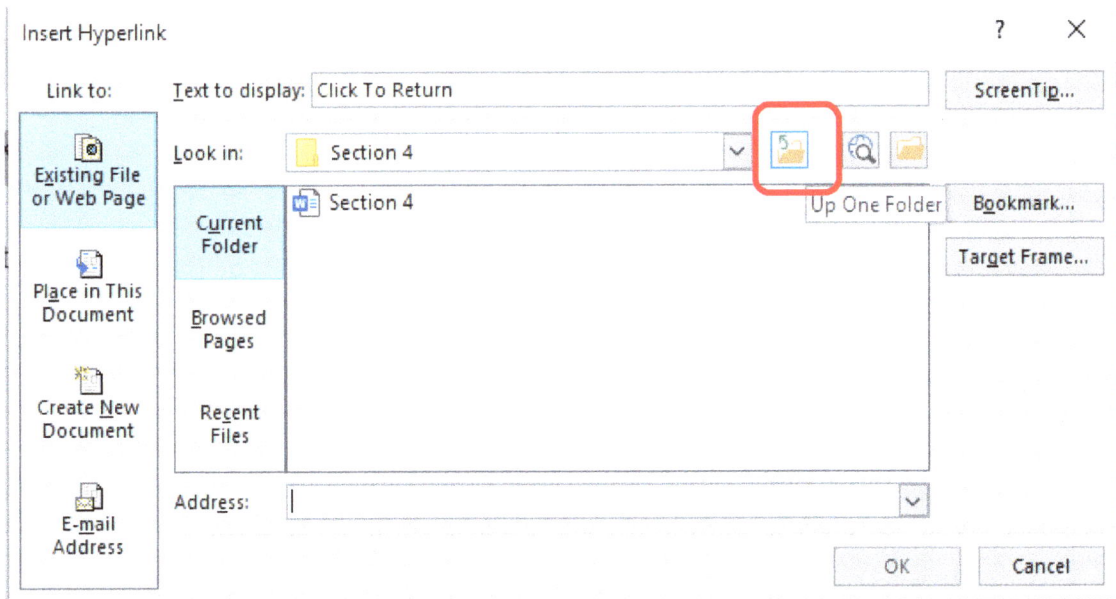

Once we can see our **Startup File**, highlight the file and select the **Bookmark** button.

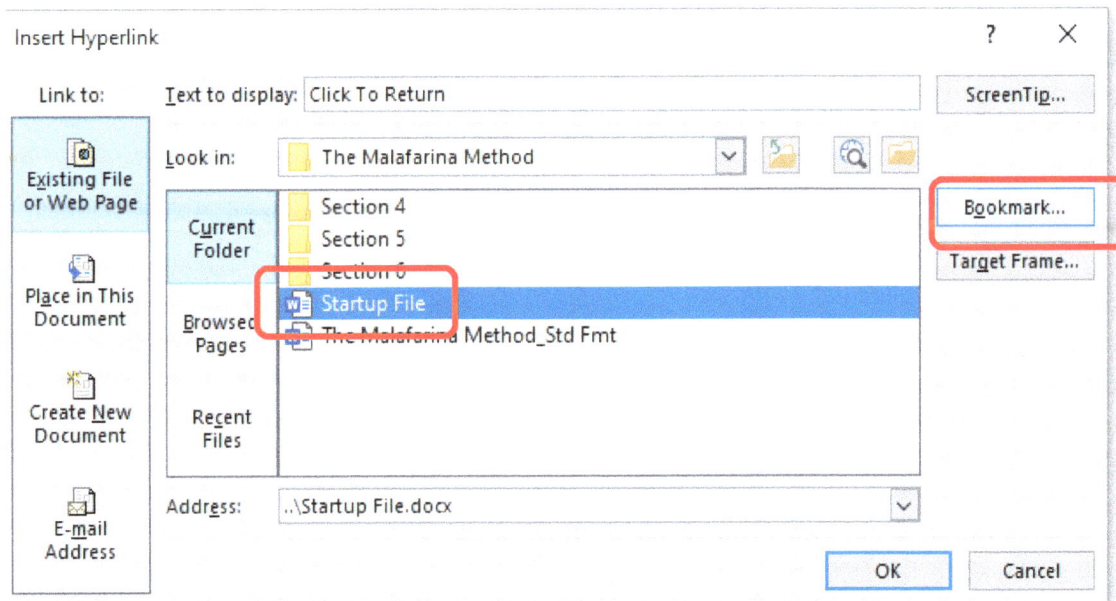

When you select the **Bookmark** button, the **Select Place In Document** window appears.

Select your bookmark **Section_4_TOC**, then click **OK**.

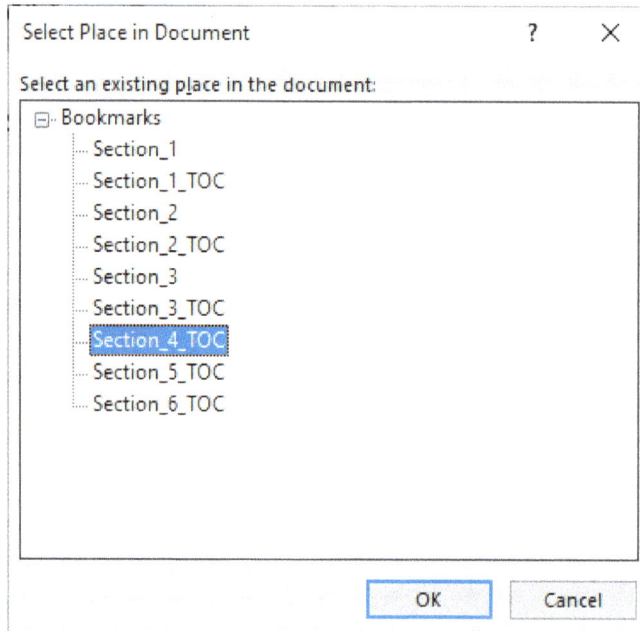

Click **OK** again to back out of the **Insert Hyperlink** window.

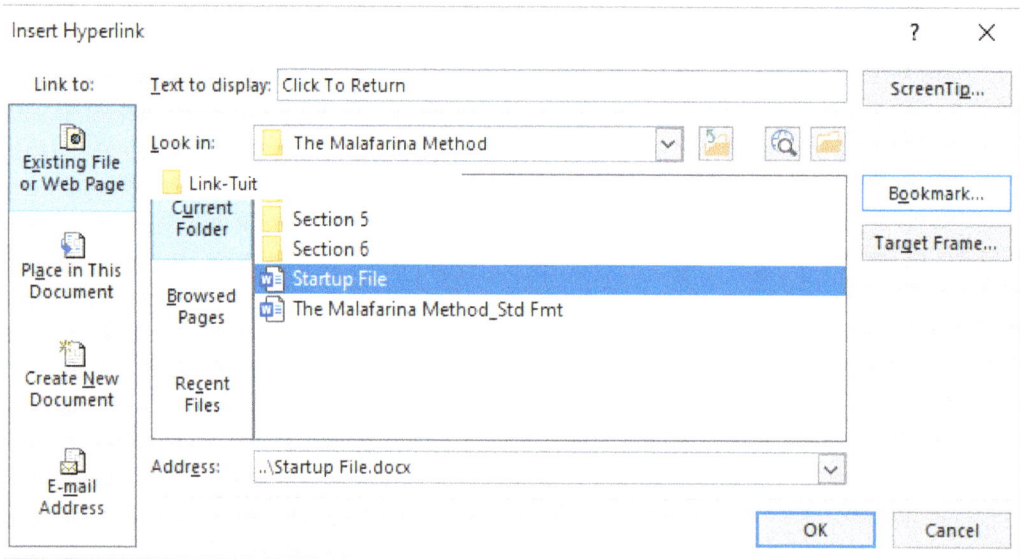

When you exit the window, you will see that a hyperlink has been created linking this **Section 4** document to the **Startup File** document.

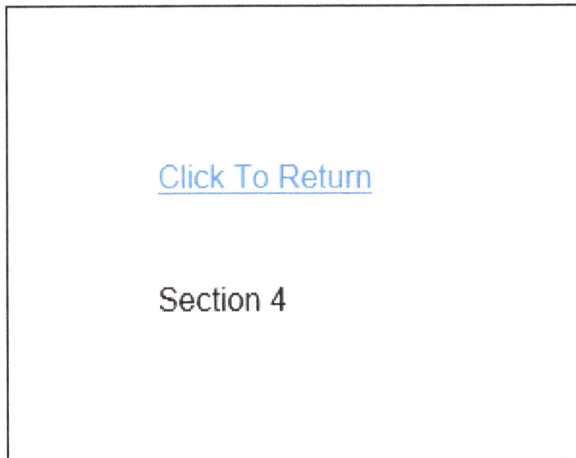

```
                Click To Return


                  Section 4
```

Click the hyperlink to see what happens.

You are transported back to the **Startup File** document with the cursor positioned at **Section 4**.

Table Of Contents

Section 1

Section 2

Section 3

Section 4 (Separate DOC)

Section 5 (Separate DOC)

Section 6 (Separate DOC)

Now, we need to create a hyperlink from the **Startup File** back to the **Section 4** document.

To do this, highlight the **Section 4** line and then select the **Add a Hyperlink** icon.

You'll notice I only highlight the words Section 4 and not the whole line. This is one of those personal preference things. You do what you like. You only have to select one letter to create the hyperlink. To each his own.

Table Of Contents

Section 1

Section 2

Section 3

Section 4 (Separate DOC)

Section 5 (Separate DOC)

Section 6 (Separate DOC)

The **Insert Hyperlink** window will appear.

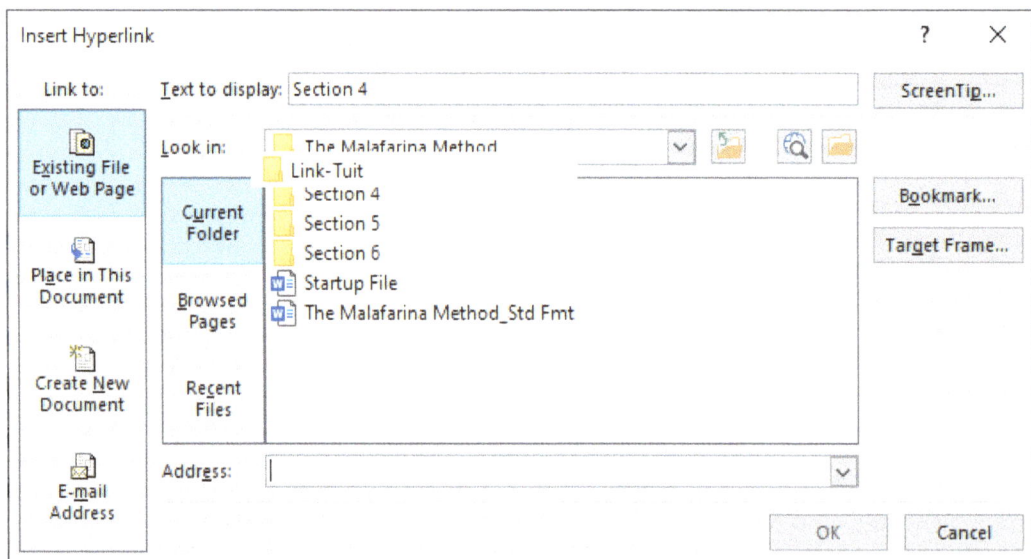

Double-click the **Section 4** subdirectory to get into that folder.

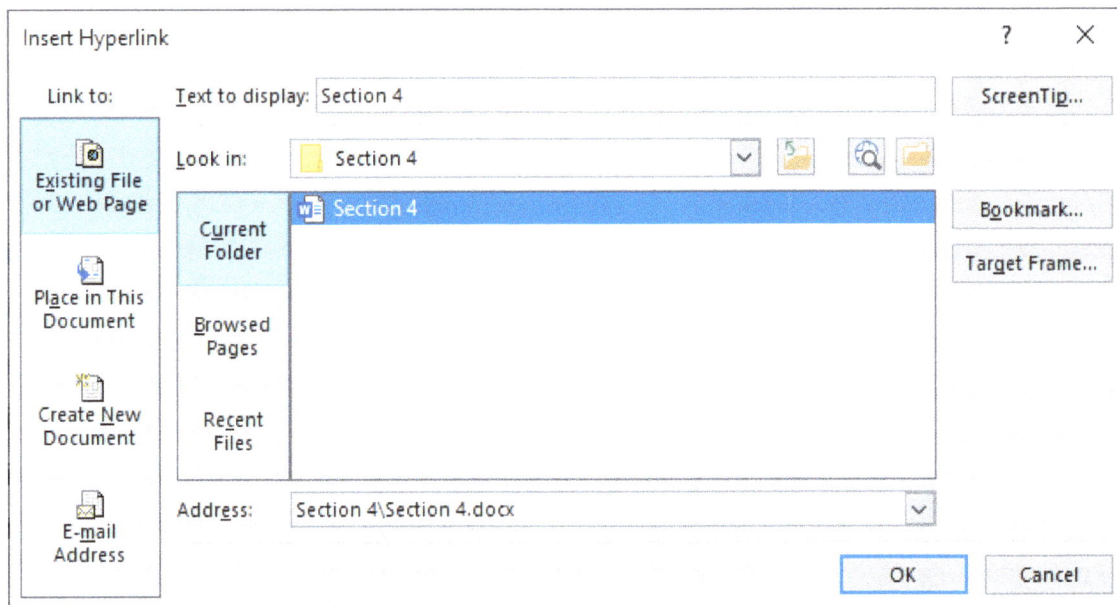

Select the **Section 4** document, and then select **OK**. There is no need to select the **Bookmark** button, as we want to enter the document at the start of the document.

When you do this, a hyperlink will be created connecting the **Startup** file to the **Section 4** document in the **Section 4** subdirectory.

Table Of Contents

Section 1

Section 2

Section 3

Section 4 (Separate DOC)

Section 5 (Separate DOC)

Section 6 (Separate DOC)

Save your file.

Now try this. Close the **Section 4** document and click on the **Section 4** hyperlink in the **Startup File** to open the **Section 4** document. Then click the **Click To Return** to return to the **Startup File**.

I do have to warn you, when you open a separate document and hyperlink back to the original document, the linked to document may remain open. You will have to close it later if you want to. I only point this out because if you start clicking on a bunch of separate documents, you can quickly find yourself with a quite a few of them open.

Now it's your turn. Do the same thing we just did with **Section 5** and **Section 6.**

Again, it may seem like a lot of work initially but if you copy, paste, and rename files then edit their hyperlinks, this goes very quickly.

I'll wait again for you to finish... hum hum hum (Jeopardy music playing in background).

Back already? Wow! You're doing great.

So now you should have a Startup file with hyperlinks that look like this:

Table Of Contents

Section 1

Section 2

Section 3

Section 4 (Separate DOC)

Section 5 (Separate DOC)

Section 6 (Separate DOC)

And you should have three files named **Section 4, Section 5** and **Section 6** all located in their proper directories that look like this:

Click To Return   Click To Return   Click To Return

Section 4   Section 5   Section 6

The hyperlinks in each of these three documents should all link back to the **Startup File**. And likewise, you should be able to open each of them from the hyperlinks in the **Startup File**.

Is everything working the way it is supposed to?

Good, you rock

One more thing. Here is special note about file names and the # sign.

Although MS Office allows you to have a file name with the pound sign (#) in it, (aka hash tag for you younger folks); it will not allow you to establish a hyperlink to a document with a # sign in it.

Actually, that is not exactly correct; it will allow you to create the hyperlink, it just won't work right.

For example, if I create a hyperlink to a file with a # sign name such as

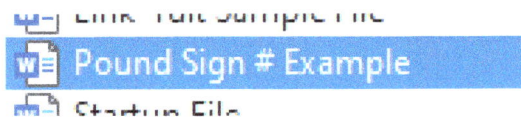

Pound Sign # Example

It will establish the hyperlink, but the link will not work.

It will give you the following error.

39

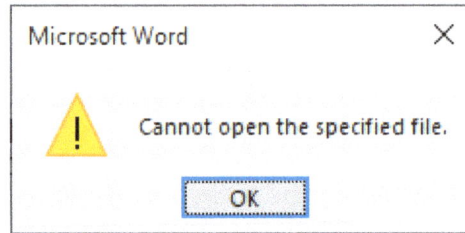

Microsoft Word   ✕

⚠ Cannot open the specified file.

OK

Solution: Rename the file and remove the #. (A stroke of genius!)

Then re-establish the hyperlink and the world will be a happy place once more.

Now on to Chapter 4.

←

Chapter 4

Subdirectory Organization

This chapter should be short because we talked for a bit about subdirectories when we created the subdirectories for **Sections 4, 5**, and **6**.

The important thing to remember is that you organize your subdirectories in a way that make sense and that you will likely not have to move or rename.
Remember how I said if you move or rename a file or subdirectory, you lose your hyperlink and have to recreate a new hyperlink?
Let's show you how this works.

Go into the **Section 4** subdirectory and rename the **Section 4** file to **Section 8**.

Open up your **Startup File**, and click on the **Section 4** hyperlink.

You get yelled at by MS Word.

Table Of Contents

Section 1

Section 2

Section 3

Section 4 (Separa

Section 5 (Separate DOC)

Section 6 (Separate DOC)

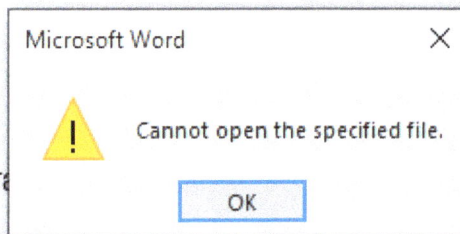

Microsoft Word   ✕

⚠   Cannot open the specified file.

OK

Fortunately, you can rename the file back to **Section 4**, and the link would be automatically reestablished.

Give it a try; rename the file back to **Section 4** and click the link in your **Startup File** again.

It worked!

Let's try something else. Rename the **Section 4** subdirectory to **Section 8**, but leave the file named **Section 4**. Then try to click on the **Section 4** hyperlink in you **Startup File** and see if it connects.

Table Of Contents

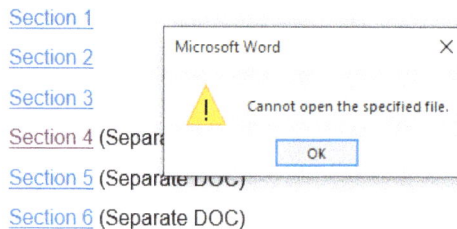

Section 1

Section 2

Section 3

Section 4 (Separa

Section 5 (Separate DOC)

Section 6 (Separate DOC)

Microsoft Word   ✕

⚠   Cannot open the specified file.

OK

Ah, our friendly neighborhood error message has returned as expected.

Rename the subdirectory back to **Section 4** and then try to click the link in your **Startup File** again.
It worked!

Ok. Let's try something else.

Move the **Section 4** file to the main directory (where the startup file is) and try to click the link in the **Startup File** to open the **Section 4** document. (We should get an error – DUH!)

Table Of Contents

Section 1

Section 2

Section 3

Section 4 (Separa

Section 5 (Separate DOC)

Section 6 (Separate DOC)

Microsoft Word   ✕

⚠   Cannot open the specified file.

OK

Bingo! It hath returned.

Now move it back to where it belongs and click the hyperlink again.

It works again! Woo-hoo!

So, we've learned that links can be established, links can be broken, and links can be reestablished.

In the event that you do lose a link and renaming or moving the file back to its original location doesn't work for you, you can always manually reestablish the link as we have done in our previous examples.

Onward and upward to Chapter 5.

Chapter 5

Linking To Excel Documents

In this chapter we'll look at linking to external Excel documents from our **Startup File.**

The process is identical to that which we've done in the previous chapters but the naming conventions I like to use changes slightly.

First, let's create a subdirectory called **Section 7**.

Then, open MS Excel and create a new Excel file. Save the file as **Section 7** in the **Section 7** directory.

Once you have saved the Excel file, close it and open the **Startup File** document. Add the following line: **Section 7 (Separate XLSX)**.

Table Of Contents

As you can see, I chose to use the Excel extension **XLSX** to identify this separate document as being an Excel document.

Now, add a hyperlink from the **Startup File** to the Excel file **Section 7** in the **Section 7** subdirectory.

It should look like this when you are finished.

Table Of Contents

I generally don't add a bookmark for any external files I link to except for MS Word documents. Again, it's my personal preference since I generally don't hyperlink back from the documents; I just close them. For example, when linking to a file that does not permit hyperlinking, the point becomes moot. If you want to add one, go for it.

Now click on the link and watch your Excel file open.

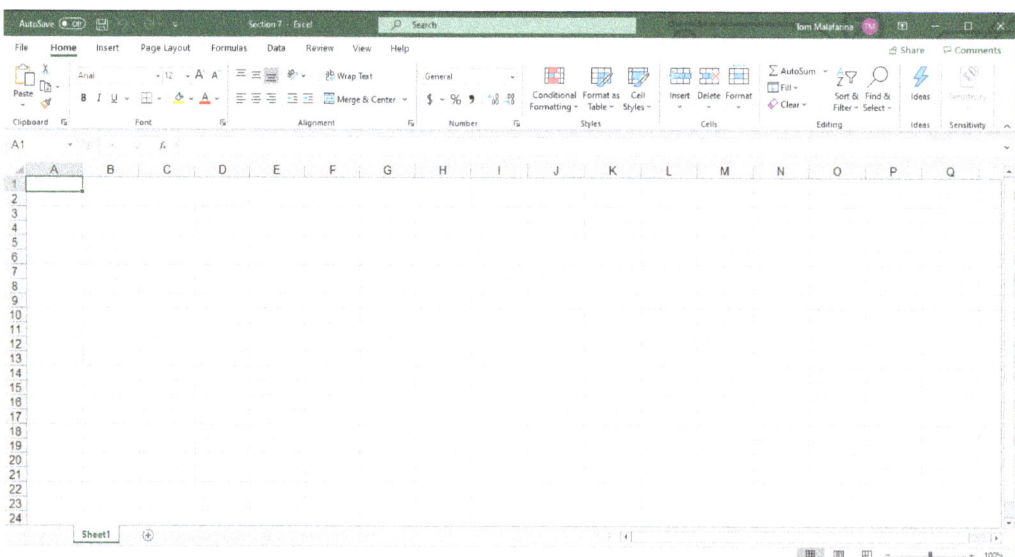

←

Chapter 6

Linking To Other External Documents and Websites

You've probably already begun thinking about how you can use this hyperlinking technique to access other external files such as PDF files, PowerPoint presentations, photos, video files, and so on. They don't have to be Microsoft documents.

The process is identical to what we did in **Chapter 5**. Again, I recommend when linking to a separate file that you identify it in some way that helps you to recognize what sort of file it is.

For example, see below:

Table Of Contents

Section 1

Section 2

Section 3

Section 4 (Separate DOC)

Section 5 (Separate DOC)

Section 6 (Separate DOC)

Section 7 (Separate XLSX)

Section 8 (Separate PPTX)

Section 9 (Separate PDF)

It works for just about anything!
If you can think of it, you can Link-Tuit.

In addition to linking to items within a document or separate documents, you can also hyperlink to websites.

Say for example you've spent a good deal of time tracking down information on the web and want a way to get back to that website quickly, just Link-Tuit.

You can make these links part of an existing document, part of your **Table of Contents**, or you can make a separate document consisting of website links.

You can link a word or phrase to a website, or you can paste the link and then click on it.

First, you need to know which website you want to connect to and what the URL is for that website. In the name of shameless self-promotion, I'll use my personal writing website for this example.

I've taken the liberty of going to the website, finding the desired page, and copying the URL from the top of the screen.

https://thomasmalafarina.wordpress.com/

If Word doesn't automatically create a hyperlink, you can create one yourself.

To hyperlink a website to a word or phrase, highlight the desired word(s) then click the **Add a Hyperlink** icon.

For example, lets type the words **Click here** and hyperlink them.

Select (Highlight) the URL for the website you want to link to such as the one above.

Then select (Highlight) the phrase **Click here** then select the **Add A Hyperlink** icon.

Click here

The **Insert Hyperlink** window will appear. Click on the **Existing File or Web Page** option.

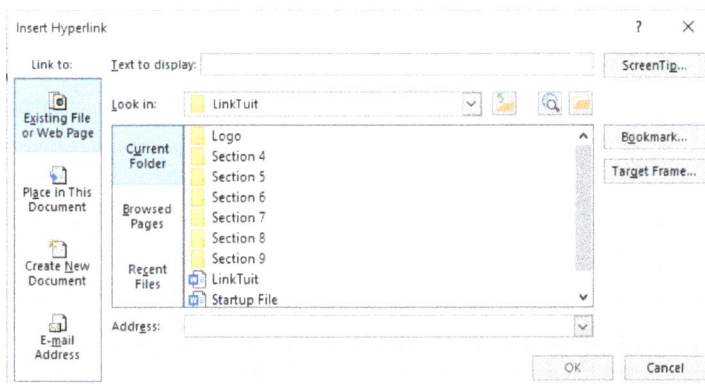

Now, down in the **Address** line, right-click and paste the URL for my website then press **OK**.

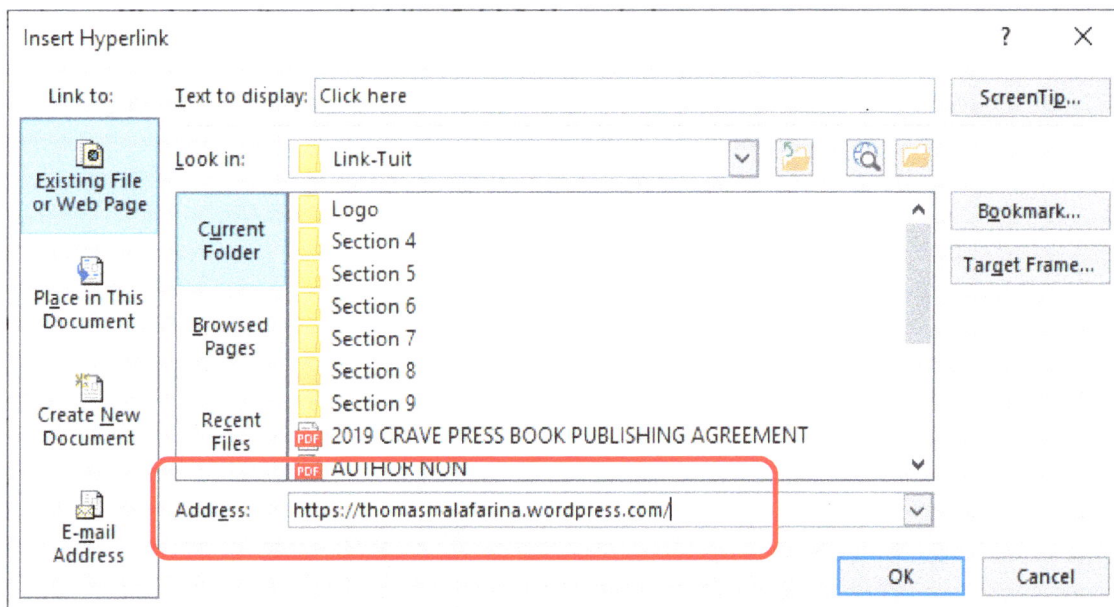

Your **Click Here** phrase will change color indicating that you have successfully created a hyperlink to my website.

Click Here

Give it a try. Click on the phrase and you will be transported to the website where you may feel free to become acquainted with as many of my books as you would like. They are available on Amazon in both dead tree version as well as Kindle. Thanks in advance… $$$$$$

As I mentioned earlier, you can also simply paste the link then when you hit space or Enter at the end of the line; most of the time it will automatically become a hyperlink.

Tom's Book Website

https://thomasmalafarina.wordpress.com/

If for some reason it does not create the hyperlink automatically, you can follow the above procedure to make it into a hyperlink.

You can also store a bunch of related website links in a separate document and link to them from your **Startup File Document**.

Table Of Contents

Section 1
Section 2
Section 3
Section 4 (Separate DOC)
Section 5 (Separate DOC)
Section 6 (Separate DOC)
Section 7 (Separate XLSX)
Section 8 (Separate PPTX)
Section 9 (Separate PDF)
Various Website Links (Separate DOC)

Click To Return

Various Website Links

Tom's Webpage Main

https://thomasmalafarina.wordpress.com/

Tom's Webpage Bibliography

https://thomasmalafarina.wordpress.com/about-2/

←

Chapter 7

Helpful Hints

We've already covered a lot of helpful hints throughout this document. I'll summarize them here and toss in a couple more.

Back in Chapter 1, we discussed how we can save time by changing the default hyperlink selector from **CTRL+ Click** to **Click only**.

We also mentioned adding the **Insert a Bookmark** and **Adding a Hyperlink** icons to your **Quick Access Toolbar**. This is a real timesaver.

We discussed setting your preferred default **Font**, otherwise you will have to change the font to what you want every time you start a new document.

Use copy and paste for both files as well as text to save time. It's easier to copy and edit a hyperlink than to do it from scratch, especially if you use a special formatting that you prefer.

Below are some additional tips we haven't already covered in detail.

Create a Blank Template Document

This concept, which I mentioned earlier, will save you some time. Creating a default template file or generic startup file can not only save you time when creating multiple documents, but it also reduces the possibility of typos. If you create a blank document (call it what you will, but I call mine "Blank") before you start compiling your notes, you can copy and paste as many copies of the blank document in your subdirectory and you will have a format already set up with the right colors and fonts to begin compiling your notes.

For example, who wants to bother selecting the title line and changing the font size and color hundreds of times? My "Blank" document is very simple. It contains a dummy hyperlink to nowhere that is formatted in red, italic, Arial, bold, Size 12. This is followed by a space then a dummy title in blue, Arial, bold, size 14. Then I have a space followed by a dummy text line in black, Arial, size 12. Generally, I add several more blank likes to assure that I have the text format continue as I add notes to the document. Here is what it looks like.

Click to Return

Title

Text

Creating Subdirectories – Planning Ahead

Organizing your file folders and subfolders in a logical manner is a good practice. It will save you time searching for folders and documents. This doesn't have as much to do with Link-Tuit as it does with planning and organizing the design of your directory and document structure. However, as you use the Link-Tuit method more and make it part of your daily routine, you will find that subdirectory organization becomes critical.

Let's say you start compiling some notes on a new software package you are learning or on a new series of procedures you company is going to use. It's irrelevant what type of software product or type of procedure you are learning; no matter what the discipline, the process is the same. It's a good idea to first get an overview of what you will be doing and then plan your subdirectories accordingly.

For example, suppose you are attending a training session about some new software package. The first thing you would want to have is an outline of what your will be learning. Here is one possible outline for an imaginary class on using MS Word.

Introduction / Overview
The MS Word Interface
The File Tab
The Home Tab
The Insert Tab
… and so on

Based on the above outline, I would assume the instruction would follow the format of the outline. Obviously, you would not be able to take notes, organize, and link your documents during the presentation. But you could take notes and, after the training was over, return to your PC and organize your subdirectories in the same way the class was organized using the Link-Tuit method.

You could have a main subdirectory called MS Word Training. Then you could have separate subdirectories for each section covered in the training. This way not only could you keep any notes separated and organized, but you would also be able to add your own notes in the appropriate subdirectories in an organized fashion over the months ahead as you continue to learn more.

Let's look at a subdirectory I would call **File Tab**. This would contain my notes from the class pertaining to the File Tab of MS Word.

First, I would have the main directory called **MS Word Training**. Within that directory, I would have an MS Word file called **MS Word Main** or **MS Word Master Document** or something you could use to identify it as the main document from which the rest of the documents will hyperlink.

It might have a table of contents that looks like the one shown below (again, it's all up to how anal you want to get with your organization). I will just list the first three sections to keep things simple.

Introduction / Overview (DIR)
      Introduction / Overview Master Document (DOC)

The MS Word Interface (DIR)
      The MS Word Interface Master Document (DOC)

The File Tab (DIR)
      The File Tab Master Document (DOC)

What this listing tells me is I have a separate subdirectory (DIR) set up for each of the sections covered in the training. I have a hyperlink set up to each directory so that if I ever want to just open up a subdirectory and see what all files are stored there, I can simply click that hyperlink and be there in a flash.

Then withing each subdirectory I have a "Master Document" (DOC) for each of the subjects covered. If I click for example on **The File Tab Master Document** hyperlink, it will open an MS Word document which could not only go into a lengthy discussion of the **File Tab** within the document itself, but it could link to other documents and files that would go into detailed explanations of the various functions of the file tab. Below is a sample of what **The File Tab Master Document** might look like with an explanation of each line in *Green* next to it.

Click to Return   *(Return hyperlink)*

The File Tab   *(Title)*

Home   *(This tells me that the description of the Home function is in this document — no external note after the link — and is hyperlinked.)*

New   *(This tells me that the description of the New function is in this document — no external note after the link — and is hyperlinked.)*

Creating A New Word Document **(PDF)** *(This tells me that there is also a separate PDF file called Creating a New Word Document — note the PDF identifier in parentheses — with no return link.)*

How to Create a Word Document **(MP4)** *(This tells me that there is also a separate MP4 Video file — note the MP4 identifier in parentheses — called How to Create a Word Document with no return link.)*

I may have mentioned this earlier, but depending upon the editing software you have for other software, it is possible to add return links to .XLSX, .PDF, .PPT and other such formats, but I never bother. For me just being able to open these files from an MS Word document is sufficient. Even I am only so anal about this stuff, but if the spirit moves you, feel free to **Link-Tuit** as you see fit.

As I hope you can see by structuring your files with different subdirectories for each section of the training, not only do you allow for organization of what you have learned in the training session, but you have also allowed for the addition of new information as you learn more. For example, the PDF file, "Creating a New Word Document" and the video file, "How to Create a Word Document" may not have been given out at the training class but might be something you found online afterward and decided you wanted to keep and access at some later date.

By organizing your data in the appropriate subdirectories and using the Link-Tuit method to hyperlink to the documents, it will be simple for you to allow your wealth of information to grow and to be able to find the information you need whenever you need it in just a few mouse clicks.

Standardization

Standardization is always a good practice and a time saver. Come up with a format you like, and stick with it. That way, if you link to a document someone else created, it will stand out as being different and not one you originated. I know that sounds a bit strange, but if multiple people within your organization are using Link-Tuit and sharing documents from a central location, it's sometimes good to know which were your files and which were not.

Broken Hyperlinks

WARNING: Be careful, and remember if you **RENAME** of **MOVE** a file or directory, your Hyperlinks will be **BROKEN** and will **NO LONGER WORK.**

Whenever you rename a file or directory be sure to **IMMEDIATELY** update any of your documents and relink and hyperlinks to these files or directories.

However, if you forget to do so, the worst that will happen is your hyperlinks will no longer work. This is not the end of the world, but it can be a pain if you are under pressure to find your information. All you need to do is reestablish the hyperlinks by relinking to the file or directory.

As I said, if you do it right away, it is better; if you wait until crunch time, you will likely be cursing yourself for not doing it earlier. Better yet, decide on you file and directory name and **DON'T CHANGE OR MOVE THEM**. You will thank yourself for it.

Set Up Hyperlinks To Online Locations

If you have a website or a collection of websites or YouTube videos which you need to reference on occasion, set up a Link-Tuit hyperlink to those URL locations.

Identifying External File Types In Your Table Of Contents

In this document, I used the words (Separate DOC) to let the user know that we were accessing a separate .doc file. Likewise, the same thing can be done with other extensions. However, it is easier, cleaner, and takes up less space if you were to simply identify the document in the table of contents as (DOC).This tells us several things. It identifies that the document being called is an MS Word Document (.doc extension). It also tells us that there is likely a return link to this document in the document to be called.

If I link to a document that already links back to a different document, I label it (DOC No Return). This tells me that I am linking to an MS Word document and that it will not return me to this document.

Below are some examples of Table Of Contents files linking to a variety of external files. You can use my abbreviations or make up your own. (You won't hurt my feelings.)

Table Of Contents

Removing Hyperlinks

From time to time, you may want to remove a hyperlink or change the document or place the hyperlink is linking to. Often you can simply highlight the link and then link to the new location and it will automatically write over the old hyperlink. However, sometimes MS Word is finicky (at least I've experienced it on occasion) and you may have to first remove the old hyperlink before creating the new hyperlink.

If you want to remove a single hyperlink you can simply right-click the link and select Remove Hyperlink from the drop-down box. You can highlight it, but right-clicking anywhere in the link does the same thing.

Then presto-change-o, the hyperlink is removed.

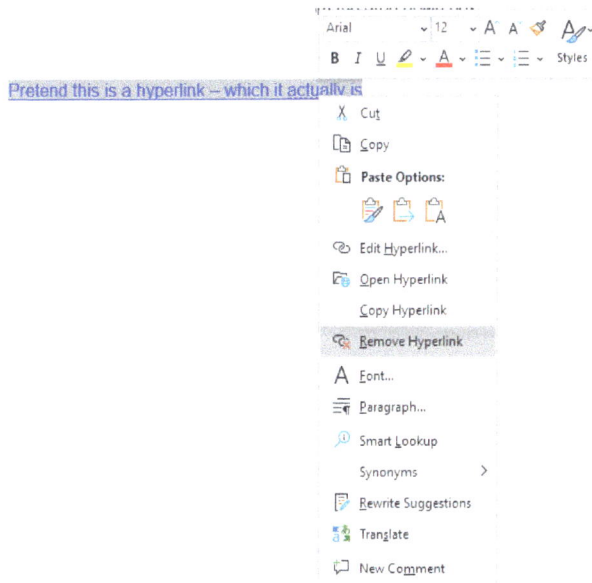

Deleting Multiple Hyperlinks

Suppose as part of your information gathering you copy several pages of information from an online document and paste it into your MS Word notes in the same format as it was online in order to grab the images and illustrations. (Is this plagiarism? Not unless you claim it as your own work. However, it probably is stealing, so it's a good idea to make a note of where you got the information from.)

So now that you've gotten your information pasted into a document, suppose you discover that the information you pasted has a ton of hyperlinks within the description that you really don't care about. In other words, you want the notes but have no desire to accidently click on a word and be sent to some place on the web.

You could individually right-click each hyperlink and remove it or to save a boat-load of time, or you could simply select and highlight the entire section of new information and press **CTRL SHIFT F9** key combination to delete all the hyperlinks at one time. Nice and neat and tidy.

Warning: Again, MS Word sometimes is finicky and although **CTRL SHIFT F9** will remove all the hyperlinks associated with the text in the document, sometimes if there are hyperlinks on the **illustrations or pictures,** some of them may not go away and sadly, you will have to remove those individually.

Chapter 8

Real World Example - Create A Linked Network Of Documents

So now that you are skilled with using the Link-Tuit method, you should be able to create a network of documents on your computer that link to all your personal and professional files.

As with all projects, **start off small**. Believe me, it will quickly grow of its own accord into a larger network.

Below is a sample chart you can use as an example to start creating your own Link-Tuit network and begin organizing your documents.

Keep in mind, this is just a generic representation only; yours may and very likely will look a lot different depending upon how you organize your computer.

Also, I have deliberately kept it VERY SIMPLE, allowing room for growth which, as I said, will most definitely come.

```
                           Main Document
                                |
        ┌───────────────────────┼───────────────────────┐
        |                       |                        |
       Home                    Work                    Music
        |                       |                        |
   ┌────┼────┐                  |                    ┌────┼────┐
   |    |    |                  |                    |    |    |
Finances Taxes Pictures         |               Musicians Bands Lyrics
                         ┌───────┼───────┐
                         |       |       |
                     Projects Technical Resume
```

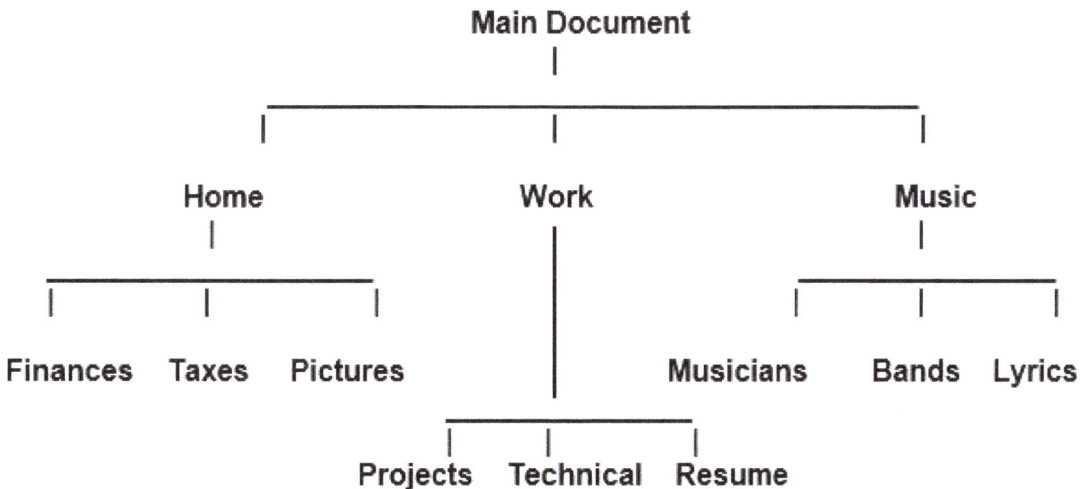

I have set this chart up with a **Main** document which I would likely store in the root directory of the computer.

Example: C:\Main Document.doc

This main document would then link to three other documents each stored in a logically named subdirectory.

Example: **C:\Home\Home.doc**

C:\Work\Work.doc

C:\Music\Music.doc

These three documents would then call other documents likewise stored in logically named subdirectories within their subdirectories.

Example: **C:\Home\Finances\Finances.doc**

C:\Home\Taxes\Taxes.doc

C:\Home\Pictures\Pictures.doc

C:\Work\Projects\Projects.doc

C:\Work\Technical\Technical.doc

C:\Work\Resume\Resume.doc

C:\Other\Music\Musicians.doc

C:\Other\Music\Bands.doc

C:\Other\Music\Lyrics.doc

And so on… and so on…

As you can see it doesn't take long until you have organized yourself to the point that you are the **Master of Efficiency**.

Ok, so you're likely saying, "Big fat hairy deal. What's so great about this and how can it help me in my day to day life?"

Here are a few scenarios you might run into if you were the person using the above example.

Imagine you are sitting at your home computer and your wife comes into the room and out of the blue tells you she needs the tax return from back in 2017 which it was your responsibility to store. Now also imagine you giving her that deer-in-the-headlights look while simultaneously she's giving you her patented, "You better not have lost them," look.

You could get out of your chair, go down into the basement, dig out the box marked "Taxes 2017," then root through the box until you found the hardcopy of your 2017 tax return.

Or, if you had digital (scanned) versions of these documents stored on your computer, you could search around your hard drive until you found them, which would be quicker. But using the Link-Tuit method, you could smugly and confidently smile at your beloved and say, "I'll have it in a second."

All you have to do is open your **Main** document, click on the **Home** hyperlink, then the **Taxes** hyperlink, then the **2017 Taxes** hyperlink, and voila, you have what you need in seconds ready to print without even getting out of your chair.

Here's another possible situation. Suppose while at work, your boss asks you, "Hey, remember back a few years ago we did that project for XYZ Corporation? I recall we had some sort of problem when with that project. Now they want us to do something similar and I want to avoid that issue if possible, whatever the heck it was. Didn't you say you were going to make a note somewhere about that in case it ever happened again? Dig those notes out and get them to me ASAP."

Oh crap! The heat is on. You know your boss can be a total jerk when he doesn't get a prompt reply. If you don't have that answer in five minutes, he'll be back asking what's taking so long, saying, "I thought you were more organized that that. I guess I was wrong. I'll have to remember that at your yearly evaluation."

You could open your file cabinet and search for the project file, then leaf through a ton of documents and hope you can find the note your scribbled to yourself five years earlier.

Or using the Link-Tuit method, you would go to your **Work** document, click on the **Projects** hyperlink which will lead you to a document that you could organize let's say by **Customers**, then click on the **XYZ Customer** hyperlink opening that document and find a listing in the table of contents that said something like **"XYZ Project Problem For Future Reference."** Click that hyperlink and proudly displayed in front of you is the digital note you wrote five years earlier. Press print, and your work is done.

Now when your lunkhead boss comes flying into your cubical, you can calmly look up at him, hand him your printed sheet, and say, "The problem was blah, blah blah." Then as he looks on in astonished amazement, you can smile, all the while thinking, "Take that, you worthless overpaid goofball."

As I mentioned earlier, I am a part time musician. And in the chart above, you'll see I included that **Music** category for purely personal reasons. I actually have many, many other categories in my personal network of Link-Tuit documents for all of my extracurricular activities. It boggles the mind.

But for now, let's look at a scenario using the Music category. Suppose you find out that due to some unforeseen problem, your band will not be able to play a gig scheduled for the following weekend. You've already called the club owner and broken the bad news to him. After he finished calling you a series of names using words you would never have heard from your mother, he tells you to find a replacement band to fill your slot or you can forget about ever playing in his club again.

As tempting as it might be to tell him to stick his threat where the sun doesn't shine, you realize that the rest of your band is depending on you to keep your cool and do the right thing.

So, using the Link-Tuit system example above, you open the **Music** document the click on the **Bands** hyperlink in the table of contents which opens the Bands document. Then you scroll down through the list of bands to find one compatible with your own and see one called **The Broken Hearted Po Boys**. You click the link to open their document and see a list of names, phone numbers, and email addresses. One phone call later you have your replacement lined up. You call the club owner and now miraculously, the vulgar name-calling has stopped, and you are back in his good graces.

As you can see, the ways you can use Link-Tuit to organize your life are virtually limitless. You can make your own network of documents as simple or as complex as you choose. It is all up to you.

Conclusion

Ok, now I've shown you enough to make you as dangerous as I am. It's your turn to take the ball and run with it. Use your imagination. Go for it. Get organized. Manage your time.

Kick the stress right out of your life. Free up your brain for more creative projects. Stop worrying about everything you formerly had to remember. Just click your way to the answers with **Link-Tuit**.

www.ingramcontent.com/pod-product-compliance
Lightning Source LLC
Chambersburg PA
CBHW061236270326
41930CB00021B/3483